Breaking Bread

By the author

Called: New Thinking on Christian Vocation

Daily We Touch Him: Practical Religious Experiences

Centering Prayer:
Renewing an Ancient Christian Prayer Form

A Place Apart: Monastic Prayer and Practice for Everyone

Monastic Journey to India

The Eucharist Yesterday and Today

In Peter's Footsteps: Learning to Be a Disciple

Jubilee: A Monk's Journal

O Holy Mountain: Journal of a Retreat on Mount Athos

In Search of True Wisdom:
Visits to Eastern Spiritual Fathers and Mothers

Challenges in Prayer

Monastery

Last of the Fathers

BREAKING BREAD

The Table Talk of Jesus

M. Basil Pennington, o.c.s.o.

1817

Harper & Row, Publishers, San Francisco
Cambridge, Hagerstown, New York, Philadelphia, Washington
London, Mexico City, São Paulo, Singapore, Sydney

FIRST EDITION

Library of Congress Cataloging-in-Publication Data

Pennington, M. Basil.
   Breaking bread.

   1. Jesus Christ—Person and offices. 2. Jesus Christ
—Words. I. Title.
BT202.P427   1986   232.9'5   85–51008
ISBN 0-06-254060-2

86 87 88 89 90 HC 10 9 8 7 6 5 4 3 2 1

To
Rabbi Lawrence Kushner
and his
family and friends
and all my
Jewish friends
who know that
God sits at their table

CONTENTS

Introduction   ix

1. This First Sign (John 2:1–11):
   The Son of a Mother   1

2. The Power of Sharing (John 6:1–15):
   Twelve Baskets of Leftovers   15

3. At Home with Sinners (Luke 5:27–32):
   He's a Winebibber and Glutton   29

4. But Not with the Just (Luke 7:36–50):
   She Has Sinned Much   35

5. The Better Part (Luke 10:38–42):
   The Bread of the Word   45

6. Wherever the Good News Is Proclaimed (John 12:1–8):
   There Is a Place for Waste   55

7. In Memory (Mark 14:22–25):
   At the Heart of It All   63

8. In the Breaking of the Bread (Luke 24:13–35):
   Were Not Our Hearts Burning?   71

9. Ghosts Don't Eat (Luke 24:36–49):
   But a Risen Savior Does   79

10. Do You Love Me? (John 21:1–22):
    A Prophecy Reversed   87

11. Side by Side (Revelation 3:14–22):
    The Consummation in the Kingdom   99

Epilogue (Mark 8:14–21):
   Not His Kind of Bread   107

INTRODUCTION

"We would see Jesus." So the two gentiles expressed their aspiration to the apostle Philip. In this, they express the deepest longing of our own hearts as Christians, followers, disciples, and lovers of Christ Jesus. Of course, we do not want just to see him; we want to hear him and know him through and through.

And we can. In deep prayer we can contact him present within us. Our faith can lead us. And our love can go beyond all that our rational minds can conceive; it can bring us into an experiential communion with him. We can, indeed, see Jesus in the way that only the eyes of love can see.

Such experience will undoubtedly create in us an even greater desire to see him on other levels also. We want to know all about him: how he thinks, how he responds, what his values are, what his promises are. We can begin to satisfy this very legitimate desire by encountering our Lord in faith in the Gospels. There is a real presence in the Word of God. He is there to speak to us and reveal himself to us. We have but to come with the eyes and ears of faith, with a listening heart.

Certain passages in the Gospels are very special. In his Sermon on the Mount, Jesus lays out in detail the panorama of his way. There are more intimate moments, like the night he sat with Nicodemus. Or that time with his Twelve on the hill overlooking Jerusalem, when his words turned to prophecy and he spoke of the fate of the city, the nation, his Church, and the world.

If we really want to get to know the thoughts of a person on a wide variety of subjects, there is, perhaps, no better way than to eavesdrop regularly on his or her meal conversations. The table invites a certain candor. Speech flows freely with the wine. Stories are told. Memories are shared. New ideas are aired. There is a generous, friendly, give-and-take. This is especially true in the Jewish tradition. Eating and drinking are considered pious and sanctifying acts in this religious culture, which has always stayed closely linked with the family hearth. There is the ritual: hands are washed, benedictions are pronounced over the various foods. There is a concluding grace appropriate to the season or the occasion. But above all, there is discussion of Torah. The tradition goes so far as to say that persons who discuss Torah during a meal "are as though they had eaten of the table of God." On the other hand, those who have not "are as though they had eaten sacrifices of the dead."

For the Jews, meals are an integral part of all the festivities of life and of the commemoration of the great moments of sacred history. Primary for them is the weekly Sabbath, marked by three *se'udah shel mitzvah*, festive religious meals. The meal that has come to have the richest traditions surrounding it is the Passover meal at the *seder*.

Recently I was specially honored with an invitation from Rabbi Lawrence to join his extended family for the *seder* meal. The Rabbi told me that, when he moved to town, he specifically selected a particular house in order to have sufficient space to lay out the long festive board. Around it some twenty-six gathered. The children (among whom I was happily counted) were seated closest to the Rabbi, with his youngest son, Zach, at his side. The evening unfolded according to the ancient ritual: hands were washed, cups were blessed, and songs were joyfully sung. And especially, Torah was shared. Little Zach asked the traditional four questions concerning the feast. The Haggadah—the Scriptural account of the first Passover—was read paragraph by paragraph around the table, interrupted by question after question and by playfully serious and seriously playful argument. Even this gentile was allowed to add his two cents. The children went off at times to play their games. Some of the guests slept a bit. There were intervening songs and wordless melodies and joyful rounds, and even games. Through it all, the lively discussion went on. I probably have never gotten so close to what a meal with the Rabbi from Nazareth must have been like as I did that festive night.

In the following pages I would like for us to sit at a table with Jesus. Let us truly enter into the spirit of the table. If we prefer, rather than being one of the invited guests, we can be one of the other characters in the scene, looking in upon the table. A bit of Halloween—we can choose whatever role we wish. In each of the chapters of this book I will choose a certain role and leave it to the reader to try another. If we truly know ourselves, our true self would be the best of guises. Most of us do not really know ourselves. We find ourselves to be rather a confusing collection of selves. Then let us try on different ones and listen to how we hear Jesus in our role as the good guy, trying hard; the lazy so-and-so; the backslider; the selfish sinner, whether hardened or repentant; the father or mother, brother or sister, friend or disciple. As we encounter Jesus in each of these, we will hear the needed "word of life" that will help us integrate all these aspects of our lives. We will come to see ourselves integrally and essentially as Jesus sees and loves us. This can be a most liberating experience for us. We can come to love ourselves truly, knowing ourselves as persons of beauty and worth. Proudly and joyfully, then, we can give ourselves in love to Jesus-God and, with him, to the Father and to all our sisters and brothers.

As we listen to Jesus, and watch him—oftentimes actions

speak louder than words—we will come to know him as a person. And to love him, for we cannot come to know a good person like him and not love him. When we come to know him and love him as a person, we will then see his acts differently. We will see them in the light of who he is. Then, because they are his acts, we will begin to be understood and accept acts which would have disconcerted us or at least seemed ambiguous. The transition point comes when we know the inmost desires of his heart. So we are going to be watching and listening, not only to know the thoughts and acts of Jesus, but to know the inmost desires of his heart. These are what we want to know and understand.

One of the great mystical writers of sixth-century Syria, the pseudo-Dionysius, said there are three kinds of contemplation. There is direct contemplation, when, illumined by the grace of the Holy Spirit, we pierce right into the divine mystery. There is oblique contemplation, when we get to know the divine through what God has created. And there is circular contemplation, when we circle around the Reality and perceive, one after the other, its many facets. We will be circling around the mystery of Christ, the divine Love, Incarnate in our midst, our Way of Truth to Life.

We want our perception to be penetrating. The Fathers tell us that there are four senses or meanings to be found in the Sacred Scriptures. There is, first of all, the literal meaning of the sacred text. This is what is means historically. Sometimes there is much work for the exegetes to do to capture the true historical sense. This sense always gives us the basic or foundational meaning. Then there are the spiritual meanings, which will be our main concern in this book. We recall how Saint Paul told us that Sarah and Hagar, literally the two wives of Abraham, were the two covenants. Jerusalem is literally a city on Mount Sion; but it is also the People of God, the Church, and the heavenly city. Beneath the literal sense, the Fathers discerned three spiritual senses. The allegorical sense gives the meaning in the order of grace: Jerusalem is the People of God. The moral sense indicates what is to be our response to this reality: as the new Jerusalem we are to act as befits the People of God. And the anagogic proclaims the ultimate meaning for us all: Jerusalem is the heavenly city. As we listen to Jesus, let us peel away the rind of literal meaning so that we can be nourished by the fruit of what lies within. Let us break open the shell of the nut so that we can eat the rich meat it encloses. These are the spiritual meanings that the Holy Spirit, who inspired the sacred writers and guided their tongues and pens, and who dwells within us, will reveal to us if we listen humbly with the inner ear of the heart.

When we sit down to listen to the Scriptures, Jesus himself breaks for us the Bread of the Word. Let us sit at his table and be nourished with the table talk of Jesus.

Note: I have placed the relevant Scripture passage at the beginning of each chapter. I would encourage you to spend some time with it before going on to my reflections. In my reflections I will draw on parallel and other passages of Scripture and use other translations that serve better to clarify my thoughts.

The Lord our God has given me
a disciple's tongue.
So that I may know how to reply to the wearied
he provides me with speech.
Each morning he wakes me to hear,
to listen like a disciple.
The Lord our God has opened my ear.

—Isaiah 50:4–5

THIS FIRST SIGN
The Son of a Mother

There was a wedding at Cana in Galilee. The mother of Jesus was there, and Jesus and his disciples had also been invited. When they ran out of wine, since the wine provided for the wedding was all finished, the mother of Jesus said to him, "They have no wine." Jesus said, "Woman, why turn to me? My hour has not come yet." His mother said to the servants, "Do whatever he tells you." There were six stone water jars standing there, meant for the ablutions that are customary among the Jews; each could hold twenty or thirty gallons. Jesus said to the servants, "Fill the jars with water," and they filled them to the brim. "Draw some out now," he told them, "and take it to the steward." They did this; the steward tasted the water, and it had turned into wine. Having no idea where it came from—only the servants who had drawn the water knew—the steward called the bridegroom and said, "People generally serve the best wine first, and keep the cheaper sort till the guests have had plenty to drink; but you have kept the best wine till now." This was the first of the signs given by Jesus: it was given at Cana of Galilee. He let his glory be seen, and his disciples believed in him.

—John 2:1-11

This first time we meet Jesus at table, we hear little by way of speech from him. This is not surprising. It is, so to speak, the debut of a new young rabbi. In fact, reading the text, we get the impression he was present among the invitees primarily because he was the son of Mary. It was she who was the friend of the family. Later, when he became a well-known rabbi, he would be a center of attraction. The people would crowd around him, and the usual rabbinical discussion would take place. But for this time, before his first "sign," he was seen largely as just one of the crowd of guests, the son of the widow from Nazareth. He was the carpenter's son, and himself a carpenter. The only ones who would have hung close to him would have been the motley crew he brought along with him. In the open and free hospitality of the East, in the village-wide celebration of a marriage, their presence would not have been out of order—though they may well have contributed to the crisis we hear about in this story.

Then, too, the occasion was probably not suitable for the teaching of a rabbi to take prominence. Other kinds of meal gatherings would be more appropriate. This was a time for celebration. And a celebration it was! All too soon it became apparent there was not going to be enough with which to celebrate. It was the keen eye of a caring mother that first noticed the coming crisis. What was to be done?

This mother knew her boy. He would know how to handle things. Saint John tells us that this was to be his first "sign." Mary approached her son, probably with no expectation of a sign. She just knew, as mothers do, that her son could take care of things. Or did she expect more? Her son's response is quite enigmatic. Commentators have had fun with it through nineteen centuries.

Some see Jesus squirming in his seat. "Well, Mother, do you really want it to go down in sacred history that the first miracle the Son of God worked here on earth was to turn out more booze for the boys after they had drunk the house dry?"

Others have seen a sort of wink going back and forth between the two, as the son makes his point for our benefit.

Some exegetes would place the emphasis on the second sentence: "My hour has not yet come." He was not disassociating her from himself and his mission, but simply did not see this as the occasion to begin to establish his credentials by his "works"—his signs. When his "hour" did arrive, she would be fully with him, even as she had been up to this time.

The question then is: Was the time advanced? Jesus would say, "Ask and you shall receive." Saint James tells us that the reason we do not receive what we ask for is that we are like the waves of the sea, fluctuating in our hearts. Mary did not waver, "Do whatever he tells you." She knew he would act.

Note here, Mary did not actually ask Jesus to do anything. She did articulate her need and concern, did lay it before him for us all to see. She articulated the concern of her heart so that we would know it. There is, in fact, no need for us to ask Jesus for things. We do not have to make a litany of all our own needs and all the other needs that press on our hearts or are commended to our prayer. The Father knows what we need. The important thing is that we do truly carry these needs in our hearts. Jesus does not listen to our lips. He listens to our hearts. There he sees our concern and our confidence—he does the rest.

Other commentators would see Jesus, here and elsewhere, treating his Mother very much as he treats us—taking away only so that he can return a hundredfold. Here, as in the Temple some eighteen years before, and as he would do soon again in a crowded house, Jesus seems to be taking away Mary's motherhood. In the Temple he said, "Why were you looking for me? Did you not know I had to be in my Father's house?" He had moved out of her family into another awesome one. Later, when others would say, "Your Mother is outside seeking you," he would reply, "Who is my mother?" But after having, as it were, taken away her motherhood, on Calvary he would give her the mothering of all those who would become one Body with him in the redemption: "Woman, behold your son."

At Cana, Jesus seems to be establishing a new, independent relationship. Up till now, he was her boy, living in her home, taking care of all her needs and errands. Now he is to be about "his own thing." He has to establish his autonomy. It is only right. Yet, there stands his Father's command: "Honor your father and mother." This is an important part of growing up: becoming autonomous and establishing a new relationship with our parents. He who was like us in all things but sin also had to work this through.

For him, this transition undoubtedly was not burdened with much of the pain we know. We have to let go of a lot of anger—after we have had the courage to admit it is there. All our parents fail. They are sinners, like the rest of the human race. But somehow, we expect our parents to be perfect and infallible.

There is the ultimate "failure," of course, when a parent dies. I remember seeing a movie entitled *Two Kinds of Love*. It told the story of a young mother who died of cancer. Her ten-year-old was very angry. He could not express his anger against her, so he turned on the father for not taking proper care of her and not forcing her to take care of herself: "When parents bring a child into the world, they have an obligation to take care of themselves so they can take care of their child."

Almost as bad is the anger toward parents who have failed to keep their marriage intact. The mounting plague of divorce is engendering an increasingly angry generation.

Gays, too, experience a special anger toward their parents. No one really knows what determines our sexual orientation—whether the cause is genetic, or environmental. But a confused and hurting adolescent hears enough about parents' being the cause; he or she cannot escape a certain anger. And the anger is greatly compounded when those parents, one way or another, make it clear they are not ready to accept a gay son or daughter.

We all share in anger toward parents. We resent it that our parents do not pass on to us the gifts and talents that others have received. We are angry because they have not better provided for us in education, parental care and guidance, wealth and opportunities, and many other things. We have to acknowledge our anger. And then let go of it. In the space opened, we can then create a new relationship. It will be a relationship in which we accept our parents as they really are. We can never thank them enough for the basic gift of life. Without them, we simply would not exist. In a society dominated by an abortion mentality, we can appreciate all the more the gift of life. Many are not receiving it. Much more was given to us beside this, no matter how deficient the sum might seem to be. We need to look at the doughnut and not be all taken up with the hole.

Along with gratitude comes the call to honor these parents whom God himself has chosen to be the first sacraments of his love in our lives, the sacraments of his parenthood.

Apart from all these special dimensions, we have here a basic human relationship, a relationship between human beings. Love and compassion call upon us to respond to our parents in all their real humanness. They supplied for many of our needs in our time of weakness. Now, when their weaknesses are laid bare and admitted—at least in our consciousness—it is time for us to begin to care for and provide for them.

Jesus probably had less cause for anger than any other son. But if he was like us in all things but sin, he did experience on certain occasions some of the anger we all experience toward our parents. In any case, it was time for him to establish a new relationship with his mother. As a now-independent child, he says no to his mother. But as an adult, caring son, he takes on her cares.

Jesus always did the things that pleased his Father. He did not always do the things that pleased his mother—at least, at a certain level. Ultimately, Mary also wanted him to do always the things that please the Father. But a mother's heart could not but be hurt—did not Simeon foretell it?—as her son lived out the will that called for a total self-giving in love. Yet through it all, always doing the things that please the Father, he would honor his mother.

What his mother seemed to be looking for now was not exactly an essential of life or even one of the big things (I do not mean to say that joy and celebration are not essentials of human life—they are, if it is to be fully human). It was not feeding the hungry, or giving sight to the blind, or raising a friend back to life. No, but it was a mother's concern. And that was enough for this loving, caring, honoring son.

We are fortunate if this mother brings our needs to that son of hers where they now dwell together. She was given to us as mother: "Behold your mother." All of us are the beloved disciples of the Lord.

My mother died a few years ago. And now when I think of her and would, as it were, rest my weary head on her bosom, I find she melds into Mary. In the oneness we have in Christ, mother and Mary are one. This may seem like a rather saccharine bit of piety to some. But we need a bit of such sweetness in our lives. Each evening, my fellow monks and I end our monastic day by singing that magnificent medieval hymn in which we join in the chorus of the ages in hailing Mary as "our life, our sweetness, and our hope." In another hymn we cry: *"Monstra te esse matrem*—Show yourself a mother." Of course, she quickly replies: *"Monstra te esse filium*—Show yourself a son!"

At this meal, the occasion of Jesus' first sign, he taught more by actions than by words. Actions speak louder. He invites us, as disciples, to ponder on how we, as responsible adults, are going to create new and appropriate relationships with our parents—relationships which honor and care, even as we maintain our due autonomy. In an age of increasing longevity, where parents are with us longer and their neediness is prolonged, this becomes more and more of a challenge for us all.

Saint Luke tells us repeatedly in his Gospel narrative how Mary herself faced the enigmatic teaching of the events of her son's life. She pondered all these things in her heart. She gives us the fruit of that pondering and of her own lived experience as she speaks her word of life in this first table encounter with Jesus: "Do whatever he tells you." She who had said, "Behold the servant of the Lord. Be it done unto me according to your word" knew from experience what could be the fruit of such a response to God: "Blessed is the fruit of your womb." In her word to us, Mary is but echoing the word of Jesus' eternal parent: "This is my beloved son. Listen to him."

As we move on from table to table, this will be our concern: to listen to him so that we can do whatever he tells us.

"There were six stone water jars standing there, meant for the ablutions. . . . Jesus said to the servants, 'Fill the jars. . . .' "

In responding to his mother, Jesus was teaching us important lessons. The way he went about satisfying the need she brought to him is itself instructive in its rich symbolism.

Jesus chose to use the large jugs that stood at the door of every proper Jewish home to provide the water needed for the ritual ablutions or purification rites. Jesus was beginning his ministry. And he chose something that belongs to the entering into a gathering. We are concerned with beginnings here. His cousin had been preparing the way for Jesus and his mission, for the inauguration of the Kingdom, by an ablution, by a baptism of water. Jesus himself had humbly submitted to John's preparatory rite. And in that very moment, the new Kingdom began to make its appearance. There we have the first manifestation of the Trinity, the central mystery of Christian faith. The Father spoke as the Son rose out of the waters, and the Spirit descended to enliven and guide the new.

The way into the Kingdom, into the fullness that Jesus was beginning to proclaim, is through an ablution which we have come to call baptism. Jesus commanded that these jars used for old ritual ablutions be filled, filled to the brim. With his kingdom comes the fullness. The fullness of ablution, of purification, of redemption, is to be found in Jesus. John had come with his preparatory rite, baptizing in water. But he promised that one more powerful than he would soon come and would baptize with something stronger. Jesus now changed the waters of ablution into wine. Later, when his disciples were prepared to understand, he would change wine into his very own blood. This would be at the supper on the night before he died. He would then institute a memorial rite that would forever, till the end of time, make present the source of our redemption, the true ablution. We are cleansed in his blood. And only in his blood. All the other rituals of purification were pointing toward this, preparing for it, and were efficacious only insofar as they participated in its power.

This blood, in which we are washed and made clean, is indeed the wine of the Kingdom. Through it, the marriage celebration between Christ and his bride, the Church, is brought to completion. His blood is the inebriating wine that brings us to the fullness of the joy of the heavenly nuptials. The end is in the beginning. It is not really by chance that the Son of Man worked his first sign at a wedding, and that it involved wine in ablution pots. There is a divine plan in it all. If we have but eyes that see and ears that truly listen we will perceive the loving hand of the Father in all; we will perceive the guiding presence of his Holy Spirit. The wedding feast at Cana in Galilee had been in the divine plan from the beginning.

" . . . but you have kept the best wine till now."

Indeed, our provident Father has kept the best till now, till these last times. He has sent the best of messengers, his very own son. Remember the story that his son told in the last week of his earthly life:

A man planted a vineyard and leased it to tenants, and went abroad for a long while. When the time came, he sent a servant to the tenants to get his share of the produce of the vineyard from them. But the tenants thrashed him, and sent him away empty-handed. But her persevered and sent a second servant; they thrashed him too and treated him shamefully and sent him away empty-handed. He still persevered and sent a third; they wounded this one also, and threw him out. Then the owner of the vineyard said, "What am I to do? I will send them my dear son. Perhaps they will respect him."

—Luke 20:9–13

At the moment of the feast at Cana, perhaps the rest of this story was not yet determined. The beloved son had come, the best of messengers. The best wine had been saved till last.

But this is true not only of the messenger, but also of the message. Certainly, God's word to his chosen people was a call to intimacy with the Lord. One has but to read the prophet Hosea or Solomon's Song of Songs. However, in this primitive call there is something very physical and earthy about the relationship they describe. The chosen people were a people; flesh and blood was important. The transcendent culmination of the relationship was hardly hinted at. It would be only with the new wine, celebrating a new covenant, that all would become manifest. "I no longer call you servants [in many ways the lover or wife had a status hardly above that of servant in regard to her man] but friends, because I have made known to you all that the Father has made known to me." This new relationship would go the full way: "Greater love than this no man has than that he lay down his life for his friends." The message is one of God's totally gratuitous, self-giving love, with a call to enter into and share the fullness of divine life and love.

One of the great undermining mores of our times is the fact that relationships in the key covenant in our society, in marriage, remain so frequently on the physical level. True friendship, the fruit of deep and intimate sharing of the inner mind and heart, is often not allowed to take place. There is no real friendship between husband and wife except where they make known to each other their truest selves. Moreover, the gift of self in intercourse, the ultimate physical expression, has, all too often, been made cheap, used thoughtlessly for passing pleasure or playful satisfaction.

When this has been the case, it can only with great difficulty become the satisfying expression of a total and profound gift between two who are covenant friends.

Certainly, in speaking rather of friendship and the intimate sharing of mind and heart, of self-giving love, and in choosing celibacy for himself, Jesus did not mean to rule out the importance of physical relations. As in all else, he came to fulfill the old. He himself did not fear physical intimacy. The disciple whom Jesus loved could rest his head on his loving Master's bosom. The "un"-faithful disciple could readily greet Jesus with a kiss. Men, as much as women, need warm affectionate relations that include due physical expressions. A distortion in our society has been a sort of hands-off policy, at least for men. It has been, Don't touch unless you want to go to bed. The freeing that has come through the outpouring of the Spirit in the charismatic experience has opened up some space here. But more is needed. There is still a lot of homophobia in our churches.

That Christian men can love men and express that love in physical ways when it is appropriate still needs to find more acceptance among us. Perhaps it is because we have not grasped the intimacy of the Eucharist that we fail to realize the full dimensions of our call to love as disciples of Christ.

" . . . his disciples believed in him."

There is a great simplicity and sobriety in the way Jesus went about producing his first sign. This will mark his work in general. He, indeed, can say to us: "Learn of me, for I am meek and humble of heart." Obviously, in this particular case there was a special reason for this simplicity and sobriety. Neither mother nor son wanted to call attention to the predicament of the bridegroom. Jesus, in his coming, did not want to show up the bankruptcy of the legalism that then prevailed in the religion of his people. He simply wanted quietly to fill up what was lacking. It would be hard-hearted opposition that would force him to speak out and show how the ancient rites, with their overlay of righteous ritual, were no longer free-flowing sources of joy for a people invited to the nuptials of the Lord. In this first sign, he was interested in strengthening the faith of those he had chosen to be his intimate disciples. He wanted to give them an insight into the meaning of his mission. If they had eyes to see and ears to hear, they would understand. In actual fact, their education would be a long, slow process, completed only through the inner teaching of the Spirit, whom Jesus would send to dwell in them.

These chosen men needed not only this faith-confirming sign. They also needed the other lesson Jesus had given here, that of establishing a new relationship with his mother. His people were a deeply enfleshed people. The ties of blood were strong. Jesus would have to call these men again from the boats of their fathers. They deeply felt leaving home and family and the few possessions that spelled security in a world where there was little or no social security. Peter would one day boldly ask, "Lord, we have left everything for your sake. What are we going to get?" Jesus had every right to reply that it was only just and proper that, when he called, one left everything. After all, it was he who gave them everything, including their very life. But Jesus respects the ordinary ways of his people. He knows the cost of the giving up. He has lived the experience of it himself. He did, indeed, become like us in all but sin. He left home and family and the instruments of a trade that spelled security. "Foxes have their dens, and birds their nests, but the Son of Man has not whereon to lay his head." Having given the example, he can well ask us to go forth and teach all nations.

Yet he makes Peter and the other disciples and all of us a remarkable offer: "He who leaves home and father and mother and sister and brother and children and wife and lands for my name's sake will receive a hundredfold in this life and life eternal." It is an offer one can hardly refuse. But many of us do. Because we do not trust him. The disciples did believe him—at least with the beginnings of faith. Other signs, inner graces, the enlightenment of the Father and, finally, the indwelling of the Spirit, would bring them to that faith where they would be able not only to lay down their lives, but to do it with joy—so confident were they that he would stand by his side of the bargain, this good Jew from Nazareth, the son of Mary. He who changed water into wine will change the water of our tears into the wine of the heavenly nuptials.

If it had been up to us to plan the advent of the Messiah and the proclamation of the Kingdom, we probably would not have chosen the first sign that Jesus did choose. We might bring forth many reasons against this choice. Take a minute and think of what you might have chosen to be Jesus' first sign. Your choice might tell you more about yourself and your understanding of Jesus and his relationship with you than it tells you about Jesus himself.

One of the reasons why we might be apt not to choose such a sign is that we do not have it all together. We tend to compartmentalize things. The spiritual is the spiritual, and the worldly is the worldly. Wine and parties do not quite fit in the same category for us as religion and spiritual teaching. Jesus knew what is in us. He knew full well our sin and misery. He was taking it all on so that it could be nailed to the cross with him and be destroyed. He also knew our greatness and our beauty, fashioned after his very own. He knew the goodness of human life, of joy and celebration, and of all the things of this creation. He knew that holiness is wholeness, that it lies within the doings and joys of everyday life. Jesus is like his Father, a "chip off the ole block"— if that is not too scandalous a way to express it. Like his Father and one with him, he looks upon the creation and knows that it is good—very, very good. His command is, "Increase and multiply." Marriage is a holy thing, raised by Christ to the sacramental order of grace. In marriage, love is invited to share with God in bringing the creation to fullness. Together, we are called to master the earth. Not in any dominating way that enslaves the potentials of the earth and subjugates and exploits them for self-aggrandizement. Rather, we are to be true masters, who know how to call forth and bring into being all the potency within, masters who allow their medium to express itself in fullness for the enjoyment and benefit of all. The Master, called forth by the loving care of a mother, allowed water to come to fullness in wine to rejoice the hearts of dear ones.

2

THE POWER OF SHARING
Twelve Baskets of Leftovers

Some time after this, Jesus went off to the other side of the Sea of Galilee—or of Tiberias—and a large crowd followed him, impressed by the signs he gave by curing the sick. Jesus climbed the hillside, and sat down there with his disciples. It was shortly before the Jewish feast of Passover.

Looking up, Jesus saw the crowds approaching and said to Philip, "Where can we buy some bread for these people to eat?" He only said this to test Philip; he himself knew exactly what he was going to do. Philip answered: "Two hundred denarii would only buy enough to give them a small piece each." One of his disciples, Andrew, Simon Peter's brother, said, "There is a small boy here with five barley loaves and two fish; but what is that between so many?" Jesus said to them, "Make the people sit down." There was plenty of grass there, and as many as five thousand men sat down. Then Jesus took the loaves, gave thanks, and gave them out to all who were sitting ready; he then did the same with the fish, giving out as much as was wanted. When they had eaten enough he said to the disciples, "Pick up the pieces left over, so that nothing gets wasted." So they picked them up, and filled twelve hampers with scraps left over from the meal of five barley loaves. The people, seeing this sign that he had given, said, "This really is the prophet who is to come into the world." Jesus, who could see they were about to come and take him by force and make him king, escaped back to the hills by himself.

—John 6:1-15

This rather unusual meal begins with an expression of our Lord's gracious humanity. He is, albeit somewhat reluctantly or haphazardly, it would seem, the host of a large number of people. Less gracious disciples suggest he just send his guests off: "Send these people away." But Jesus' concern will not allow that, "lest they faint on the way." Jesus knows what he is going to do. He has also decided he will use the opportunity to teach and form his disciples. He asks Philip a testing question: "Where can we buy some bread for these people to eat?"

Philip doesn't really pass the test. It is consoling for us latter-day disciples to see how much these first ones chosen by the Lord himself are like us. Philip responds much the way we do most of the time. We are very rational, very clear. We take inventory of what we have and of what is needed, and we come to a clear, well-thought-out conclusion. Jesus does expect us to use to the full the gifts he has given us, our talents and our resources. But when he asks the impossible, it is time to bring the little we do have to him so that the impossible can be done.

Today, in many ways, God is asking the impossible of his people. To live a full Christian life in a society that works on other principles demands heroic faith and courage. At first blush, it would seem to be a course that can lead only to the bottom of the heap. How can one get ahead in this world following Gospel principles? There is no rational answer to that. The person of faith can only say, "Try it and see." The result in any particular case may well be a Paschal experience—some real dying before one arises. It takes faith to go through such an experience. Sooner or later we all do have to die, and perhaps many times in many ways. "Unless you take up your cross *daily*, you cannot be my disciple." We seem to be caught in the vise of great godless economic forces that are more intent on power than on the well-being of peoples. Yet it is an economy that is leading to world disaster as lines of credit are stretched beyond the credible, poor nations become poorer and poorer, and rich nations become more and more burdened with the debts of high living, colossal waste, and nuclear-war chests.

Ultimately, we are called as Christians to have that faith and trust and love that can enable us to face and live through even a nuclear holocaust and to support our sisters and brothers in such a catastrophe. Saint Peter, who seems to describe such a disaster in the last chapter of his Second Epistle, assures us it will be followed by a new heaven and a new earth. If we survive, we will need faith and hope to go on, working with God in creating that new heaven and new earth. And we will need love to reach out to others and support them in their faith and hope.

Through all of this, confronted by our inability to bring forth some clear, rational solution to the deteriorating world situation and by the weakness of our faith, we have to learn to cry out in heartfelt prayer, "Lord, I believe. Help my unbelief."

What little we have in spiritual resources does not seem to be enough to produce peace in a world so divided into warring camps, whether those divisions are among the superpowers, among the emerging nations, among the various races, or among and within the many religions. We can catalog the struggles on fronts around the world: South Africa, North Ireland, the Near East, the nearer Caribbean, Afghanistan, Grenada, and on and on. What can we do? Where can we begin?

We can, of course, begin by creating in our own hearts the trust that brings peace: trust in God and trust in others. With this trust, we can begin to engender trust around us. We can do our little to be a bit of leaven in the lump. And we can pray. God, from within, can change our hearts. Proportionately few of the greater economic forces use their power and potential to create the sources of peace and human well-being. If only a small portion of the genius and funding that is being poured into armament research were turned toward research for a peace-oriented economy, it could perhaps be the trim tab that would begin to turn around the powerful economic forces of this world. When we begin to see that an economy of benevolence, sharing, and human services can ultimately be most profitable for human society as a whole, we can perhaps escape our present entrapment in an economy oriented toward the weapons of war. We can pray that God will touch the hearts of those who wield economic power and inspire them to begin courageously to charter a new course for the world.

"There is a small boy here with five barley loaves and two fish; but what are they between so many?"

Here is a little fellow who has a little. Andrew even notes that it is the rather inferior sort of bread made out of barley. The little man could have clung to his little. Little people, whether little physically or psychologically, tend to be rather defensive in a world of bigger people. If the little man had hung on to his little bit, it would hardly have been enough for him—and there never would have been the super bonus of twelve baskets at the end. In fact, he probably would not have been lucky enough to hang on to what he had. Bigger people would have quickly let their hunger overcome their justice. After all, a little fellow does not have as much need as a big one. We know only too well the story of such oppression. Certainly there would be envy of the little fellow who was well provided while his neighbors hungered. How prone we all are to forget or ignore our hungering neighbors while we are well fed! How often do we think of Haiti or Mexico or even the street people in our own city, as we sit down to a steak dinner? Rivalry inevitably ensues when all are not equally provided. The favor of the well-provided is curried by those who have less. Those who are stronger undertake to protect the weaker. Of course, as protectors they take what they want—first choice. How much of the history of Central America is reflected in this?

Courageously, in what was really a great act of faith, the little fellow handed over all he had to the Lord. As the disciple carried his basket to the Rabbi, the boy had no way of knowing whether he would get even a morsel. After all, the Master could have easily eaten it all himself. To sacrifice for the Master would have its own reward. And the Master did have those special twelve—big hungry men. What chance did a little guy like him have of getting anything? The little man had used what little he had in the best way possible, turning it over to the Lord in trust, for the benefit of all. And his little did the impossible. It fed five thousand men, plus probably as many women and many children—including our little fellow. He ate his fill, all he could want. So did everybody else. And in the end there was that amazing problem of twelve full baskets. (I have always wondered where those hampers came from.) How was the little fellow ever to get all that home?

Who is the Lord to whom we hand over the little we have? Spiritually, it is Jesus himself. Each day we do well to make a morning offering, giving him all that we are and all that we have—all that he has given us. An open docility that allows the Holy Spirit to guide us, coupled with detachment from our own designs and plans, is the beginning. But in the actual course of the day's unfolding, who is the Lord? It is everyone, and above all, his least ones. In giving to each other, in sharing with each other, we give to the Lord.

How much do we give? The boy gave all he had. Jesus praised the widow who gave little—two mites, but it was her all. It was not out of her superfluity; it was of her substance. We begin to make a difference when we share not only what is left over or extra, but when we share even what we ourselves need and hunger for. The little boy was hungry. Yet he gave all. We make a difference when we give ourselves, our time, the precious sands of our life. That is what we most need, all of us. We are poor; we hunger for the love, the care, and the respect of others. The bread Jesus gave that day, he was to point out, was but a symbol, as was the manna his Father had given. (He is the Son of his Father.) It was a symbol of the Bread he would give that is his very self.

4   We all belong to organizations: communities, churches, businesses. Here are places where we can begin to give ourselves for others. We can raise our voices and bring our organizations to a social consciousness so that they will begin to share insofar as they can. We can go on, as individuals and as groups, to support legislation that will move our nation to a more caring and generous sharing, both at home and abroad. We can become a sharing people, a people who act according to the reality that the whole human family is one family. We are all children of one Father, who has given the earth and all its goods to us all for the benefit of all. Report after report has affirmed that there is enough food in the world to feed everyone. This is true of all the other human needs: there is more than enough. Our Father is truly bounteous in his provision. It is a problem of distribution, of political will. We can work and pray for the resolution of this problem. And our churches can take a lead and set an example, as we Christians, giving all to the Lord, reach out across the world to Christ in our needy brothers and sisters.

"Make the people sit down."

One of the other accounts tells us Jesus had the people sit in groups of fifty—that is how they got a count of the guests. A little order is not a bad thing. It does not prevent real relationships, celebration, and joy. Chaotic spontaneity is not the only way to live and celebrate life. Order can facilitate and create context as well as multiply resources.

There comes to my mind's eye the joyous scene at the S.H.A.R.E. warehouses on distribution day. Deacon Carl Shelton's superb organizational skills have enabled hundreds of thousands of poorer people in many cities, by a pooling of their resources, to multiply them for a better living for all. His plan is basically quite simple. Each participant contributes twelve dollars and two hours of labor a month. The gathered funds purchase immense quantities of food in bulk at greatly reduced prices. The donated labor repackages the food so that each participant walks off with seventy or eighty pounds of mixed produce, including all the staples. You should see the carnival joy as the hundreds of families and friends walk away from the warehouses with their bulging bags. Organization makes the difference here, but organization rooted in love and caring and sharing.

Jesus cared. He was about to serve up a banquet. He wanted his guests to be comfortable. The place he had chosen was an unusual one in the Holy Land—there was a lot of grass there. They could sit comfortably and not have to worry about swirling dust as they enjoyed their meal. It takes a little extra effort and planning, the effort and planning that come from love, to create a beautiful environment for our ministry to the poor. I think of Mother Teresa's Homes for the Dying. They are very poor and simple, but they are always clean and bright—made brighter by the smiles and love of the sisters and brothers. Jesus always has a great reverence for the dignity of the persons he has made. He serves us graciously.

I remember a story Mother Teresa told me. It is her practice when she is home in Calcutta to go out in the early morning with the sisters. They go to the train stations and gather up the abandoned dying who had been left there during the night. One day they found an old woman, very ravaged. She would not live long. Mother claimed the privilege of caring for her. Mother did all she could to make this poor dying woman comfortable. She stayed close by, soothing her as best she could. In the last moments, the woman opened her eyes, looked into Mother's eyes, and said simply, "Thank you." And she died. Mother remained prostrate on her knees and wept. She knew what a privilege it is to serve the Lord, and this woman was her Lord. She knew who had said to her, God's humblest servant, "Thank you." Yes, it is the Lord we serve in each other. It is the indwelling Spirit, who Jesus promised would teach us all things, who teaches us by an inner instinct to know this. We serve the Lord because this is his beloved child, made in his image, participating in his nature and sharing his life. In serving people we serve the Lord, because he has intimately identified himself with his least ones. We want to serve with reverence and graciousness, in as fitting an environment as possible.

Jesus invited them to sit. Sitting is the posture of those who are served. It is also the posture for receiving. Jesus has told us that unless we become as little ones, we cannot hope to enter into his kingdom. We do not want to try to stand on our own two feet with God. We do want to be conscious of our great dignity. We are children and heirs. We do share his divine nature and life. We do have a responsibility to live according to our dignity and gifts, to use them well. This is the way we express our gratitude to the Giver. But before God we are always the recipients. We are the children who joyfully receive all from our Father with expectation and gratitude. The Lord will give to us to the extent that we are sitting, ready to receive.

"Then Jesus took the loaves, gave thanks, and gave them out to all who were sitting ready."

"Jesus gave thanks." He is, of course, the source of all that is. It is he who created this bread he holds in his hand. He invites us here into something of the deepest mystery of the Trinity. Jesus is one with his Father. There is only one God. Jesus is absolutely one with the Father, the source of all that is. And yet there is that wonderful relationship. He is the Son of the Father. He constantly acknowledges his Father as his source. "All that I have comes from the Father." Again, what an example for any adult son or daughter! Jesus loses none of his equality or dignity in graciously acknowledging his Father as father and in thanking him for all that he has given him.

This is one of the few times we see Jesus at a meal as host. As host, he takes on his due responsibility to give voice to the common prayer. The meal does not begin without a blessing, a word of thanks to the Provider. Grace before meals is a wonderful Christian practice that we have received from our forebears, our Jewish ancestors. Jesus gives thanks as a Jew, according to the practice and customs of his people.

The Jewish tradition is very rich in table blessings. Here is a beautiful one, translated and adapted for our times by the Community of Beth El in Sudbury, Massachusetts:

My friends, let us praise God!

Praise God now and forever!

With your consent, then, let us praise our God from whose abundance we have eaten.

Praise God from whose abundance we have eaten and by whose goodness we live.

Praise God, praise God!

Holy One of Blessings, Your Presence fills creation. You nourish the world with goodness and sustain it with grace, loving kindness and mercy. You provide food for every living thing because you are merciful. Because of your great goodness, the earth yields its fruit. For your sake we pray that we shall always have enough to eat, for you sustain and strengthen all that lives and provide food for the life that you created. Holy One of Blessings, you nourish all that lives.

We thank you, God, for the good land that you gave to our parents as a heritage; for liberating us from the soft slavery of Egypt; for the Covenant you sealed in our flesh; for the Torah that you teach us; for the laws that you reveal to us; for the life that you have given us and for the food which nourishes and strengthens us each day; even as it does right now.

We thank you, God, for all your gifts and praise you, as all who live must praise you each day; for you teach us in your Torah: "When you have eaten your fill, you shall praise God for the good land that God has given you." Holy One of Blessings, we thank you for the land and its fruit.

O God, have compassion on Israel, your people; on Jerusalem, your city; on Zion, the home of your glory; on the royal house of David, your anointed, and upon the great and holy Temple that was called by your name. Dear God, tend us, nourish us, sustain us and support us; and, dear God, relieve us soon from all our troubles. O God, let us never depend upon the charity of our fellows, but let us depend on your generous help, alone, so that we may never be put to shame.

Holy One of Blessings, your presence fills creation. You are our Redeemer, our Maker, our Holy One, the Holy One of Jacob. You are the Shepherd of Israel, the good Sovereign, who does good for all. As you do good each day, so, we pray, do good things for us. As you provide for us each day, so, we pray, treat us with loving kindness and compassion, relieve us from our troubles and grant us prosperity and redemption, consolation, sustenance and mercy: a good and peaceful life. Never withhold your goodness from us.

May our compassionate God rule over us now and forever!

O compassionate God, you are praised in the heavens as you are praised on earth.

O compassionate God, you will be praised by every generation and you will be honored among us forever.

May our compassionate God let us earn our living in an honorable way.

May our compassionate God deliver us from oppression and give us freedom.

THE POWER OF SHARING / 25

May our compassionate God bless this house and all who have shared our meal.

May our compassionate God send Elijah, the prophet, may he be remembered for good, to bring us the good news of redemption and consolation.

May our compassionate God bless us and all who are dear to us with the perfect blessing that God bestowed on our parents, Abraham and Sarah, Isaac and Rebecca, and Jacob, Leah and Rachel.

May we be worthy of peace, O God, and the blessings of justice from the God of our salvation and may we find grace and understanding in the sight of God and all peoples.

May our compassionate God find us worthy of the Messiah and of life in the world to come. You are a tower of strength to your king and are compassionate to your anointed, David, and his descendants now and forever. May God, who makes peace on high, bring peace to us and to all Israel.

Fear God, you holy ones, for those who fear God will feel no want. Even the strong may lack hunger but those who seek God will lack nothing that is good. Let us thank you, O God, for you are good, your compassion endures forever. You open your hand and satisfy every living thing with favor. You, who trust God, are blessed for God will protect you. I have been young and now I am old, yet never have I seen the righteous abandon those who lack bread. God will give strength to his people. God will bless her people with grace.

Grace, of course, need not be expressed in a traditional formula, though there are beautiful formulas for many of the special feasts and occasions of life. It can be quite spontaneous, adapted by the host to the gathering, as at this divine picnic, or a family celebration, or just the everydayness of the particular meal. It can be very simple. We do not know if Jesus said anything here, or simply held the bread, raised his eyes to heaven, and then broke and shared the gift. He may well have used the following *baraka* that has become familiar to the Christian community from its inclusion in some of our Eucharistic meals:

Blessed are you, Lord God of the Universe, for from your goodness we have this bread to eat, fruit of the earth and labor of human hands. May it be for us a bread of life. Blessed be God forever.

The most important part of thanksgiving is sharing. In Jewish homes, the blessing always includes the breaking and sharing of the bread held during the blessing. It is good to actually do this, really share among ourselves and symbolically express our desire to share with all our sisters and brothers everywhere. We want to cultivate in ourselves a sharing attitude.

"Pick up the pieces left over, so that nothing gets wasted."

Waste is certainly one of the greatest problems of our labor-efficient, highly technological society. We are a throwaway society. Time is, of course, of the greatest value. It is our precious life, allotted to each of us in a very limited quantity. We want to use it well. But we do use a lot of it in ways that are perhaps not as productive and re-creative as are some programs to cut down waste or recycle our resources. It has been interesting to see, in the Northeast of the United States, one state after the other adopt the so-called bottle law. The good environmental concern about so much litter has led the states to legislate incentives to get people to recycle bottles and cans. People saw the value of a more beautiful environment with sufficient clarity to raise the common consciousness. This consciousness led to the judgment that it was worth investing the time and money to preserve that environment.

We need to see clearly how important it is to use well all the gifts our Father has given us for the good of us all. Then we will take care to gather up the fragments, even if it does take a little extra time and energy. We will recycle things. When we can no longer use them, we will see if we cannot make them available to others who can use them. One example: Our American hospitals do not find it economically valuable to sterilize and reuse many things in ways that they used to. Food for the Poor gathers up these disposables and sends them on to poor clinics in the Caribbean. There they will be sterilized and reused many, many times. We will all probably find occasions when we can pass things on to the Saint Vincent de Paul Society, the Salvation Army, or the Catholic Worker instead of dumping them more conveniently into the garbage. Our recycling can perhaps make life a little more comfortable, a little more beautiful for another—another who is Christ, our Lord.

3

AT HOME WITH SINNERS
He's a Winebibber and Glutton

Jesus noticed a tax collector, Levi by name, sitting by the customs house, and said to him, "Follow me." And leaving everything he got up and followed him.

In his honor Levi held a great reception in his house, and with them at table was a large gathering of tax collectors and others. The Pharisees and their scribes complained to his disciples and said, "Why do you eat and drink with tax collectors and sinners?" Jesus said to them in reply, "It is not those who are well who need the doctor, but the sick. I have not come to call the virtuous, but sinners to repentance."

—Luke 5:27–32

"You can tell a man by the company he keeps." We have all heard this old saying. So when we see Jesus at table with friends, we look around curiously and try to get more insight into him by looking at his companions.

Others did the same. As Jesus' popularity grew and he worked more signs, the number of his enemies also grew. They began to look for every opportunity to discredit him. It would always be impossible to find anything on which they could truly fault him. But what about his companions? Here he would give them ample material for their grist mills.

Guilt by association is still one of the banes of our communities even after the experience of Jesus. How many priests shy away from ministry in certain places or to certain people, fearing this guilt by association? Let a Christian spend evenings in the bars, listening compassionately to the people gathered there and ministering to men and women who perhaps rarely if ever show up at the Sunday services. How quickly the tongues in the parish will begin to wag about this winebibber! Let a priest or religious reach out in ministry to the gay community. He or she will be labeled "gay" in very short order. A priest who talks to a prostitute is suspect immediately. Yet who is going to bring the Good News to her and invite her to the sacrament of reconciliation? After the experience of Jesus, could we not hope that things would be otherwise?

Jesus did not fear the wagging of tongues. He reached out to sinners and to all those who because of social prejudices were looked down upon and in some way considered sinners or unclean. In a religious culture that had grown shallow and legalistic, externals were valued more than internals. Undoubtedly there was a lot of corruption in the tax system. A man committed to stand against oppression would probably never take the job of tax collector (though conceivably one might do so to shield his people and make the oppression as tolerable as possible). We do not know what kind of tax collector Matthew Levi was. One doesn't have to be a saint, clearly en route to heaven, to be called by Jesus even to close fellowship and responsible discipleship. Saul the persecutor, breathing self-righteous wrath, was called. A proud and blustery Peter was called. So a tax collector was called, whatever might be his merits or lack of them. He was obviously a large-hearted sort of fellow, to throw this party. He wanted to share his good fortune with others. Can one blame him for his choice of companions? If the righteous mores of the community required good people to shun him because of his profession, where else was he to find companionship? A person needs friends and companionship. Can we condemn gays for spending their evenings in the bars when they find so little welcome in our Church gatherings and social events?

This particular gathering might have been very consciously chosen by Matthew, host and disciple. He and his new Master might even have planned the event together. Yes, a man can be known by the company he keeps. But there is more than one way to understand this saying. Besides guilt by association, there is the witness of mission. As Jesus himself put it, "It is the sick who need the physician, not the healthy—the righteous." Have we, his disciples, spent too much of our time in the company of the righteous, and not enough time in the company of the sinners and the segregated minorities?

The Church has strongly affirmed an option for the poor. Jesus certainly showed a special compassion for the poor. But as we consider the tables at which he sat, we do not find many of them among the poor. He probably did not feed many poor in those great picnics of his. But all were welcome. If Jesus showed an option in his ministry it is for the marginated, those who suffer social discrimination. He eats with tax collectors. He lets prostitutes wash his feet. He touches lepers. If he were gathering his disciples today in our country he would undoubtedly include Blacks, Hispanics, Haitians, gays, and alcoholics. This Suffering Servant, who would become so disfigured by the blight of our sin, has a special compassion on those whom society brands.

You can tell a man by the company he keeps. You can tell Jesus' great compassion by the company he chose. In the light of that, is there any reason why we sinners should hesitate to draw near to him—even though he be our very God, all holy? Holiness has been defined, at times, as meaning "set apart." No! Holiness means wholeness. Holy persons have achieved a certain integrity. In them there is consonance between who they are, as images of God, and the way they hold themselves. Always true to their inner reality, they need not be apart. They can be in the midst without fear. Where there is not love, they bring love. Where there is not innocence, they bring innocence. They are instruments of peace.

For a moment sit among the guests at Matthew's feast. The sinners are probably prostitutes, pimps, and profiteers who get along at the expense of their own people. How do you feel sitting among them? A bit uncomfortable?

Why is that?

Is it because of the kind of people they are?

Or is it more because of the people outside who are shaking their heads and wagging their fingers, asking, "Why do you eat and drink with tax collectors and sinners?"

Do you think you would be more comfortable out there, standing in the midst of that group?

Or would you feel most comfortable in a third group that would look on at the motley crowd inside and at the finger-wagging critics outside, and perhaps feel superior to them all?

Where was Jesus, your Master?

I think we would want to be with the motley crowd inside that was rejoicing at Jesus' presence in their midst. They perhaps did not understand all that was going on. But for them, there was joy in seeing one of their own honored by Jesus. There was joy in being with the man of the hour, a joy that was all the sweeter because they were usually left out of the common joys of the people.

Their joy might have been even further increased by the finger-wagging outside. But we, with Jesus, would probably want to have a certain compassion for those poor, harping critics. They were the more blind and needy on this occasion. When Jesus hung from the cross and, from his position of eminence, looked out on all those who had played a part in putting him there, his prayer was: "Father, forgive them. They do not know what they are doing." There is very little real malice in this world of ours, but a lot of blindness. We get terribly narrow and distorted conceptions of what is good—for ourselves and others. Then we pursue it with a certain righteousness. We just do not see, and do not realize that we do not see.

Jesus' Father had said long before, through his prophet Isaiah: "My thoughts are not your thoughts, nor my ways your ways; but as high as are the heavens above the earth, so are my ways above your ways and my thoughts beyond your thoughts." We keep creating some false god, one made to our own image and likeness, who sees things the way we see them and judges things the way we judge them. Our god does not like to see Jesus and his disciples sitting with prostitutes, drinking and having a good time. But that is where Jesus and his disciples are—and having a good time. Are we disciples of Jesus?

It would be good if our churches and our other communities would open their doors and truly welcome the tax collectors, and the sinners, the handicapped and the gays, and all the other minorities (not to speak of accepting women and men as equals). Too often, such a welcome is extended only if they will be "converted" and agree to be like us. The prostitutes must give up their employment. The gays must not speak about their orientation but must consider themselves privileged to be accepted among us straights. Blacks must act like whites and know how fortunate they are. How about an unconditional welcome? I do not think Jesus went to Levi's home with conditions attached. Jesus ate and drank with sinners—not former sinners or converted sinners, but sinners. Such an unconditional welcome, such a manifestation of truly Christlike love, probably would lead to some deep reconciliation and conversion—on the part of ourselves as well as of our guests. We can begin acting like our Master (if we would be true disciples) and let him take care of the afterwards.

If we would go all the way, and fully be his disciples, welcoming will not be enough. Like him, we will need to step out into the midst of tax collectors and sinners, be identified with them, suffer the finger-shaking and head-wagging. This is the Christianity we have seen in Saint Dorothy Day (if I may be so bold as to jump a bit ahead of the official Church) and among the Catholic Workers and many other groups of dedicated followers of our Master.

How many of those tax collectors and sinners who dined with Jesus that evening were truly converted? We have no way of knowing. I rather suspect that they all were, but perhaps not in the way we would have dictated or even recognized. Perhaps some kindness, gentleness, and caring came into the life of a prostitute as she went on plying her trade. Perhaps a tax collector became a bit of a Robin Hood. Who knows what seeds of grace eventually sprang up to life eternal? Did not Jesus say something about prostitutes (he didn't say ex-prostitutes) getting into the kingdom of heaven before the righteous? It is going to be interesting to see who are our table companions at the heavenly banquet!

4

BUT NOT WITH THE JUST
She Has Sinned Much

One of the Pharisees invited Jesus to a meal. When he arrived at the Pharisee's house and took his place at table, a woman came in, who had a bad name in the town. She had heard he was dining with the Pharisee and had brought with her an alabaster jar of ointment. She waited behind him at his feet, weeping, and her tears fell on his feet, and she wiped them away with her hair; then she covered his feet with kisses and anointed them with the ointment.

When the Pharisee who had invited him saw this, he said to himself, "If this man were a prophet, he would know who this woman is that is touching him and what a bad name she has." Then Jesus took him up and said, "Simon, I have something to say to you." "Speak, Master," was the reply. "There was once a creditor who had two men in his debt; one owed him five hundred denarii, the other fifty. They were unable to pay, so he pardoned them both. Which of them will love him more?" "The one who was pardoned more, I suppose," answered Simon. Jesus said, "You are right."

Then he turned to the woman. "Simon," he said, "you see this woman? I came into your house, and you poured no water over my feet, but she has poured out her tears over my feet and wiped them away with her hair. You gave me no kiss, but she has been covering my feet with kisses ever since I came in. You did not anoint my head with oil, but she has anointed my feet with ointment. For this reason I tell you that her sins, her many sins, must have been forgiven her, or she would not have shown such great love. It is the man who is forgiven little who shows little love." Then he said to her, *"Your sins are forgiven."* Those who were with him at table began to say to themselves, *"Who is this man, that he even forgives sins?"* But he said to the woman, *"Your faith has saved you; go in peace."*

—Luke 7:36–50

Jesus was a good Jew. He grew up in a good home. His life was full of ritual. Some of it came from Torah. Much of it came from the customs and practices of his ancestors. Jesus liked the ritual and observed it. Such observance was a part of good manners; it brought a certain reverence and dignity to life—provided always, of course, that a due order was observed and first things were kept first. That did not always happen. "The Sabbath is for you, not you for the Sabbath." When Jesus himself was to be host at a significant meal, he sent ahead two of his chief disciples to prepare things and to see that everything was in its appointed place. There is holiness, as well as wholeness, in preparing and offering gracious hospitality.

Simon the Pharisee invited Jesus to share a meal in his home. Jesus was the man of the hour. It would bring a certain note to Simon's home, make it the center of attraction for the moment. Yet one must not go too far. Simon would indicate his superiority by a certain rudeness.

We have seen at Cana how large pots of water were set at the entrance of the house for purification. A host would show the greatest of honor if he himself would wash the feet of his guests as they arrived. A wealthy person might mitigate this honor a bit if he stood there in welcome while his servants did the actual washing. More often, the host would simply offer the water as he greeted his arriving friends, and they would wash their own feet. This was the minimum of common courtesy. An added feature, appropriate to the special occasion, would be to anoint the guest with sweet-smelling ointments.

I shall never forget the day I was invited to dine in the home of an architect in India. He came in a car for me. As we reached the village, we had to alight, for the car could not pass through its narrow streets. The streets had been swept and decorated with designs traced in white powder on the sand. When we reached the architect's humble one-room house, a carpet was spread before the door. A bench was set on it and covered with colorful cloths. I was bidden to be seated. My host was quickly at my feet, his children bringing water and a basin. My feet were well washed and then anointed with ointments and sandalwood paste. Flowers were hung around my neck and more ointment applied to my forehead and hair. Then I was escorted into the little home. It was all very foreign to me, but one thing I did know: I was very, very welcome as a highly honored guest.

Simon did none of this for Jesus. If he did feel a twinge of remorse at his lack of due hospitality, he probably felt a gratifying justification when a prostitute suddenly fell at the Master's feet and started to make up for what he had failed to do. Is there not a tendency in us to use the perceived failures in others as an excuse for our failures toward them? We have to remember that we will not be judged on what others do, even on what they do to us. We will be judged on what we do to others. In fact, others are never diminished by our rudeness or lack of respect. We are the ones who are diminished, and if we be honest, diminished even in our own eyes, for so acting.

"Simon, I have something to say to you."

It is not surprising that the harlot was able to find her way to Jesus' feet. Jewish homes, like most Eastern homes, are remarkably open, especially on the occasion of an event like this feast for the well-known rabbi. People would be milling all around. It was such onlookers who challenged Jesus' disciples at Levi's feast. It was easy enough, then, for the prostitute to make her way in. Most would have been surprised to see her enter—it was not the sort of thing that someone like her would ordinarily do. She would usually be in other places, looking for customers. Still, no one would have stopped her here. In fact, they would have drawn back, seeking to avoid any possible contact with her, for that might lead to ritual uncleanness. It might have disturbed the host to see her there—it could cast aspersions on the house—if she had not headed directly to the guest and clung to his feet. She could reach his feet without difficulty for, at a meal, the men would be reclining on couches, their heads and shoulders toward the center where the food would be served, their feet perhaps even reaching into the crowd of onlookers.

Jesus did not let Simon's failure pass by. We do not do our brothers and sisters a favor when we gloss over their failures. When we ourselves are the ones who suffer because of such persons, it is more difficult and more delicate to call them to account. But true love calls for fraternal or sisterly correction. It must be fraternal or sisterly correction. They must know that we are to them as brother or sister, that the correction comes out of that kind of caring love. Jesus waited for the appropriate moment. He did not speak out of hurt or anger or reaction. He spoke out of love and a desire to help his host grow. "Simon, I have something to say to you."

"Your sins are forgiven."

Jesus made it clear that this woman's sins had already been forgiven her. Just when this had happened, we do not know. But her sins, her many sins, had been forgiven. This is why she loved much and came to express her love. Perhaps the moment of forgiveness came when the Master walked the streets of her town. Their eyes could have met, and that would have been enough. How powerful the eyes of Jesus must have been! His call was magnetic. We can remember how a glance from him finally brought about in Peter the great conversion that turned a blustery braggart into a humble and courageous disciple.

I have in my cell a remarkable icon. It is a head of Christ painted by the famous Pansillos. It depicts this glance of Jesus toward the denying Peter. Every time I enter my cell, the Master is there to direct that powerful glance toward me. At times I am tempted to get rid of the icon, for it is a call to weep bitterly, like Peter, over my betrayals. But always my tears turn and become like this woman's, tears of love and joy. For his saving glance is more powerful than a two-edged sword. It pierces to the depths and cuts away the deceptions. It heals. It unites. It creates joy and love.

Wherever, whenever it was, this woman had experienced that saving glance. So she comes this evening, with her alabaster jar of ointment, not to lure customers, but to give all. Those lips that had beguiled so many for gold now sought to express the very pouring out of her life's spirit at the feet of her new-found Master. Her acts were a desperate endeavor, in the ways most familiar to her, to express gratitude and love. Jesus accepted them for what they were. Each of us, being who we are, with our own proper life experience, has our own way of expressing our love. Jesus will accept whatever way we choose. All he wants is the sincere love and gratitude of our poor hearts.

This good woman had already been forgiven. But Jesus now speaks the words of absolution: "Your sins are forgiven." Jesus knows us, knows us as no one else does. After all, he made us. He knows our very human need to hear the words of absolution, our need to hear a human voice say to us in God's name: "Your sins are forgiven you."

This was the first gift of the Risen Lord. After he had greeted the Eleven behind their locked doors, he breathed upon them and gave them this sign of peace: "Whose sins you shall forgive, they are forgiven them." The more ancient Christian Communions, the Roman Catholic and the Orthodox, have understood this to be the moment of the institution of the sacrament of reconciliation or penance or confession. They believe Jesus gave to the apostles, and through them to all their successors, the power to speak, in Jesus' name, the words of divine forgiveness, just as he did this evening in the Pharisee's house. Others ask: "Who can forgive sins but God?"

Whatever be the sacramental understanding of the Risen Lord's words, I do believe they can be applied to all Christians. We are all Christ, by virtue of our identification with him through baptism. In his name we can say one to the other, "Your sins are forgiven." In our forgiving, Christ forgives, for he has so identified himself with us.

There is another side to this, a terrible one. Jesus did go on to say that Easter night, "Whose sins you shall retain, they are retained." In refusing to forgive our sister or brother, what do we do to them? Do we leave them with the crushing burden of their sin? But what Christian can dare do this? Did not our Master teach us to pray to our Father: "Forgive us our sins as we forgive those who have sinned against us"? If we dare *not* to forgive, we find ourselves constantly praying that God will not forgive us! Who can go to heaven, to the heavenly banquet, without forgiving? How could that kingdom of love be without total forgiveness on the part of all?

Stories are *in* today. And that is good. For Jesus, our Master, did much of his teaching by means of stories. Here he seeks to teach Simon with a little story about two debtors. Undoubtedly, the proud Pharisee thought he had little for which to ask God's forgiveness. In comparison to this prostitute, his account was nil. I do not think Jesus meant to endorse such an appraisal. But he was speaking to Simon in a way in which the Pharisee could hear. That is the art of good teaching. Jesus was not saying Simon had less for which to be forgiven. Nor was he saying it is good to have lots for which to be forgiven, so we should go out and sin heartily.

Thérèse of Lisieux, who lived an exceptionally sinless life, sought to interpret Jesus' story with one of her own. It went something like this. An eminent surgeon had two little daughters. One of the daughters, walking down the front path, stumbled over a stone and shattered her leg. The loving father employed his skills to the very best of his ability to care for her. In the end her healing was complete. At the same time the father saw his other little daughter coming down the path. He rushed ahead of her and removed the dangerous stone, so that she could safely go on her way. Did the father love the second child any less than the first?

It is a good question. Usually when we do have the occasion to lavish more time, attention and effort on someone, we do come to love that person more. And that love is reciprocated. This is why, when we proudly stand on our own two feet, we deprive ourselves of much love.

In any case, I do not think that is quite the point of Thérèse's story. Her point is that one can show as much love in preventing a fall as in healing it. And as much gratitude and love is due in return for the favor shown. We may not be great sinners. But we need to realize that, at least in imagination, thought, and desire, we are quite capable of every sin there is. When we see the drunk in the gutter, the prostitute on the corner, the racketeer's or arms-dealer's name in the newspaper, we can truly say: There but for the grace of God go I. Jesus made it clear that it is what comes out of the heart that makes the difference.

This is why Thomas Merton used to be just as concerned about the violence of the peacemakers as he was about the violence of the armsmakers against whom they were witnessing. The one form of violence is as much against the Spirit of God and the human spirit as is the other. In fact, as great as is the burden laid upon the human spirit by the mounting stockpiles of destructive weapons, that spirit suffers even more from the increasingly common abusive violence done by parents and spouses. If all parents were sacraments of the heavenly Parent's love, there would be no armaments, no capitalistic or communistic oppression or aggression. We would be one human family, living together in love. Each of us, then, can begin in our own homes and communities, receiving the healing love of God and bestowing it on others. Then we will have more Reverend Martin Luther Kings and Mother Teresas.

In the little story Jesus shared with Simon, he was stating a reality. The more conscious we are of our being forgiven, the more grateful and loving we will be. The very least offense on our part against the infinitely good God has something infinitely wrong about it. Comparing, then, the debt one sinner owes with that owed by another sinner becomes a bit ridiculous. How can we compare the infinite with the infinite and find any difference? We all live under the burden of needing more forgiveness than we can comprehend.

If we know ourselves, we know that the seven capital sins are well rooted within us. Thanks be to God, they do not all shoot up at the same time, at least not ordinarily. We have our moments and seasons of anger and lust. And our moments of awareness when we perceive how all that we do is veined with pride and envy. We are bonded by these deeply rooted sins and seek the freedom of the children of God. Gluttony does not take just the form of shoveling large quantities of food into our mouths, especially in our slim-is-beautiful society. We can be as much caught up by the type of our food, the quality and preparation and timing, as we can by the quantity. Again, our ambition may drive us on to long hours of exhausting labor in our field of excellence, but our sloth can show up in the lazy way we reach for the television or newspaper when we should be searching the Scriptures or sitting in silent prayer to hear the Word of God. Or our covetousness can drive us to keep up with the Joneses or outdo them with home and car and television.

Blessed and free are the poor in spirit. How grateful we will be when we are freed from all these bonds! What cause we will have to love the Lord!

"Go in peace."

Forgiveness needs not only to be given. It must also be accepted. That means we must also forgive ourselves. The pride that is so deeply rooted in us is reluctant to do this. For before we can forgive ourselves, we must first admit to ourselves the full extent of our guilt or failure. We cannot accept forgiveness for what we do not acknowledge needs forgiveness. Lack of faith inhibits our willingness to face our guilt. If we do not have a real faith in the Lord as our Savior and Redeemer, the one who can free us from our sin, our guilt, our failure, then they confront us as being irremediable. With the humility to accept the dependence of needing a redeemer, we can open ourselves to the healing love of redemption.

From this comes the courage and freedom to heed Saint Paul's admonition: "Forget what is behind, and press on." We can forget it, for it is all taken care of by our Redeemer. We can forgive and forget and go on in peace and joy.

In experiencing Christ's healing love, fully accepted, we find the freedom and the empowerment of a new beginning, one enriched by the wisdom that has been gained by our past failures. We begin to understand Augustine's boldness when, to Saint Paul's "For those who love God, all things work together unto good," he added, *"even sin."*

We can go in peace only when we have forgiven ourselves and accepted the forgiveness of others and, above all, the forgiveness of God.

5

THE BETTER PART
The Bread of the Word

*Jesus came to a village, and a woman named Martha welcomed him
into her house. She had a sister called Mary, who sat down at the
Lord's feet and listened to him speaking. Now Martha who was dis-
tracted with all the serving said, "Lord, do you not care that my sister is leaving me to do the serving all by myself? Please tell her to
help me." But the Lord answered: "Martha, Martha," he said, "you
worry and fret about so many things, and yet few are needed, indeed
only one. It is Mary who has chosen the better part; it is not to be
taken from her."*

—Luke 10:38–42

Who is this "Mary," sister of Martha? She is indeed Mary of
Bethany. But is she also Mary of Magdala? And/or the woman we met in our last chapter, the sinful woman who
washed the feet of Jesus in Simon's house? The Fathers
have varied in their opinions. Some see only one Mary—it
is the same woman who appears in all three stories. She is
the Magdalen, out of whom the Lord cast seven devils. She
comes in gratitude to Simon's house to pour out her devotion upon her Savior. Then she returns to her brother and
sister in Bethany. Others hold for three "Marys." There is
no clear basis in the Gospel accounts to assert that these

three stories speak of the same woman. The similarities are not that compelling.

Lex orandi, lex credendi. "The way we pray is the way we are to believe." The faith of the Christian community is expressed in its communal worship. The common prayer is a powerful witness to what is commonly believed. Until recently, the liturgy of the Roman Catholic Church seemed to point to one Mary. On the Feast of Saint Mary Magdalen (July 22), Roman Catholics honored the sister of Martha, the woman who washed Jesus' feet with her tears and anointed him with costly ointment both in Simon's house at the time of her conversion and later in her own home in Bethany. With the renewal of the liturgy, after the Second Vatican Council, the Roman Church has moved closer to the Byzantine tradition. As in the Orthodox Church, Mary of Bethany is now honored on July 29 with her sister, Martha, and their brother, Lazarus, while a feast is still celebrated in both communions on July 22 for Saint Mary Magdalen.

There seem to be, then, two Marys: Mary of Magdala and Mary of Bethany. I think there are some indications that this may well be the case. We never hear of the Magdalen weeping, washing, or anointing, while the other Mary is ever about this very womanly expression of affection. Whether it be at Simon's house or at Bethany, she is at Jesus' feet. There is something very curious about the household in Bethany. Remember, we are in a culture where it was all but mandatory to marry. In fact, it was a divine command: "Increase and multiply." Moreover, every woman harbored the hope that she might mother the Messiah or at least be in the line of mothers who would bring him forth to the people—although the more common belief would have limited this hope to those of the house of David. Yet here, in the sophisticated suburb of Bethany, close by the capital, we find an apparently well-known and well-to-do household where there are three unmarried siblings. Might we conjecture that Mary was indeed the sinful woman who had brought such disgrace upon the family that her sister and brother were held back from marriage? What then can be said for their love and compassion when, after their sister's conversion, they welcomed her back into the family home? I wonder if this is not why this household was so apparently a favorite of the Lord's. He who is the God of all compassion has a special love for the compassionate.

In any case, we find him this day at home with Martha and Mary.

" . . . few are needed, indeed only one."

The house was honored in its Guest. And Martha was busy about many things, agitated, even unnerved. She spoke out, perhaps feeling a bit sorry for herself—and a bit envious of her sister, so apparently favored. Jesus' response can bear two meanings. In the prophetic spirit that is his, in that profound, multi-level, enigmatic way in which he taught, he probably intended both. The obvious one is that of the gracious Guest: "Don't fuss over me, Martha. Whatever is at hand. One dish is plenty." But then, he might have been speaking on a deeper level: "All the doings and not-doings are not the issue, Martha. Only one thing is really necessary to do."

And what is that?

There is nothing you and I can do for the Lord that he could not get someone else to do. He could raise up sons and daughters to Abraham out of the field stones and give them the talent, the inspiration, and the grace to carry out all our tasks. There is only one thing that you and I can give to the Lord that absolutely no one else can ever give him. He dreamed about it, as it were, from all eternity, when he thought of creating us. If we do not give it to him, he will never get it. In this he has made himself a beggar. For he truly wants what we have to give, yet he can get it only if we decide freely to give it to him. What is this one thing—the one thing necessary? It is our personal love. This is what God made us for: to lavish the joy of his love upon us, which can be received only with love, the love that returns to him our personal love. No one else can ever give him our personal love. If we do not give it to him, he will never receive this particular love—which he wants!

This love is everything. As Saint Augustine said, "Love and do what you will." For he knew the truth of what Jesus himself had said: "He who loves me keeps my commandments." What else can love do, but what the Beloved wants? On the other hand, anything done without that love counts for naught with a God who is Love.

"It is Mary who has chosen the better part."

Traditionally, this word of the Lord has been brought forth to proclaim the superiority of the contemplative way of life over that of the active. The Marys are those who go apart and sit quietly at the feet of the Lord. The Marthas are those who are out and about, doing the things that need to be done to care for the Body of Christ. Many of the Fathers have written long passages about Martha and Mary and their respective roles. But in recent years, the comparative interpretation has been denied, or at least set aside.

Be that as it may, there is something for us all here. We can hear our Lord's word as proclaiming the importance of feeding the spirit—indeed, giving it a priority over feeding the body. A certain frugality in our provisions for everyday life—"few are needed"—will leave us with more freedom and space for the things of the Spirit. If we do not want to become spiritually emaciated, we need to feed our lives regularly with the Word of God, listening to Jesus and receiving his Revelation. This is the way we are raised to a higher level of consciousness, one consonant with the participation in the divine life we received at baptism. In this sense, the Lord is pointing to "the better part." I am sure our Lord is not encouraging us to compartmentalize our lives or urging us to evaluate our activities according to some abstract scale. No, what he wants is a totally integrated life, one lived in a way that is wholly consonant with who we are. But to live this way in practice, most of us will have to set aside time to sit, like Mary, at Jesus' feet and learn from our Master.

If we do find ourselves worrying and fretting about many things, it is probably an indication that we have not been sitting at the Master's feet. We are forgetting his words: "Be not solicitous for what you will eat, or what you will wear. Your heavenly Father knows you have need of all these things. See the birds of the air. See the lilies of the field." When we choose to be all taken up with our doings and lose the context of creative love, then we certainly are not choosing the better part. Each of us needs to know by experience how much time we need to spend sitting like Mary at our Master's feet, listening—be it to the Words of Revelation or to the sounds of silence and love—in order not to lose touch with Reality. The "better part" we want to choose is to live according to our true nature and being, as women and men who have been baptized into the Christ and made partakers of divine life and love.

What I am speaking of here is a contemplative attitude— one that allows Reality to speak to us in all its fullness.

We can certainly sympathize with Martha. She has, literally, the most important man in the world in her home, at her table. Moreover, in Eastern style, the whole village (or so it would seem to Martha) was looking on as she cared for her Guest. Can you imagine how you might be worrying and fretting as you prepared to welcome such a Guest into your home under such circumstances?

My niece and her fiancé are preparing for their marriage. They have been doing so for some months. This usually very carefree young lady is indeed worrying and fretting about many things. Don't we all, about so many things?

How often do we rehearse in our minds the details of an important meeting or some cherished plan? It distracts us from what is at hand. It saps our energies. It might even lead to sleepless nights or wearying dreams.

A contemplative attitude frees us from this. It allows us to be attentive to the "now" and not waste and weary ourselves on the past or future, which live only in our imaginations. With this attitude, we tend to what is at hand; we are peacefully present to all the depth of beauty and goodness in each least thing. When we are in touch with this reality, we realize that one thing can indeed be enough. We allow it to be present in all its magnificence. Its beauty, its giftedness can fill all the space of our consciousness. How exquisitely the contemplative spirit of traditional Oriental cultures set forth the simple things! Think of a Japanese tea or floral arrangement.

I do not mean by this to exclude all planning. The Book of Proverbs says: "One who plans a thing, succeeds." There is a time and place for planning. When the time and place arrive, it is the "now," and we should be wholly present to the planning. It is the preoccupation, the worry, the fretting that is not useful but rather counterproductive.

How do we cultivate this contemplative attitude? How do we find such freedom?

By meditation.

If we allow each thing its own due time and space in our lives, this will, of course, mean reducing the number of things in our lives. Then each thing can reveal its own beauty and integrity. We can trust it to care for itself. It will be present with all its reality. It will more than suffice.

There is a more radical way, and a more effective, quicker, and more complete way, to come to this. This is by attending to the Source of all the particular realities—persons and doings and things—that fill our lives. If, through meditation that goes to the Source of all, we come to attune our perception to what is at the center of each and every person and thing, we will constantly be in the presence not only of the fullness of each but of God, with his creative, caring love that brings each to fullness.

What I speak of here, this *centering*, can be cultivated by regular meditation of a contemplative nature. Such meditation gradually transforms our consciousness and brings us great freedom and peace as well as, or through, a deeper, truer and more complete perception of all reality.

"It is not to be taken from her."

What was Mary's reaction to Martha's carping? Mary had to live with Martha constantly. Martha may well have been Mary's older sister. And there may have been that added fact of Martha's compassionate forgiveness of a sinful past. Humanly speaking, there was a lot of pressure on Mary to conform. Or at least to feel guilty for not conforming. Had Mary, who had lost all and refound it only in Jesus, arrived at that state of self-possession that enabled her to be peacefully who she was and to do what she knew she should do?

I am blessed with many remarkable friends. Among them is a monk named Jean-Marie Déchanet. When Jean was young, he sought to enter the Benedictine abbey of Saint André de Bruges. At first he was denied entrance as a novice because of his frail health. His persistent knocking secured for him only the place of an oblate. After he had spent five successful years in the regular life, the community relented and let him become a monk. Saint André is a scholarly community. Each monk finds his appropriate subject of study. Jean undertook the immense task of preparing a critical edition of the works of William of Saint Thierry, a twelfth-century Benedictine-Cistercian whose writings, unlike those of his more brilliant friend, Bernard of Clairvaux, were relatively unknown or accepted.

Within the spirituality of William, Jean learned something about the yoking of the *anima* and the *animus*. This opened the way for him to investigate Yoga, which became a vitalizing force in his life. He became a pioneer in Christian Yoga. Such a novel path was not quite acceptable in the large traditional abbey in Belgium, so Jean soon found himself in their primitive African priory. Here he found many disciples. In time, concerned about his influence even there, the superiors gave him permission to retire to an eremitical life in the French Alps. There he lives ten months of the year in the greatest of solitude, often totally cut off by snow from all others. But during the summer months, thousands come to him to learn about Christian Yoga. The frail candidate, still quite robust as he approaches ninety (having said the *De profundis* for all those who worried about his frailty when he was a postulant), recently published his autobiography. In it he states, "We must be true to ourselves. That takes courage!"

This is something we all need to learn: to be true to ourselves—our better selves, as my first spiritual father would say. True to our true self. We need to come to know who we truly are, that uniquely beautiful person that God has made us. And to have the courage to live accordingly. Each of us is a unique expression of the divine goodness and beauty. If we do not live that and express it in our lives, it will never be expressed in this world for the glory of God and the upbuilding of the whole Body of Christ. On the journey of life, one of our first goals must be to come to know ourselves and possess ourselves. For only when we truly possess ourselves can we give ourselves in love. To give ourselves, who we truly are, to give ourselves in love to God and to our sisters and brothers—this is the one thing necessary. Mary sensed the call of Jesus. She knew her place. She rested there, content. Let others complain about her inactivity, goad her to be productive. She would be who she was called to be and do what she was called to do. This is the better part. And her Lord would come to her defense. "It is not to be taken from her."

And what about Martha? She, too, had her role. She had a task to fulfill. She was to take care of the Body of Jesus. It is an important task. It is not to be shirked, even on the pretense of choosing "the better part." The responsibility lies with each of us to fulfill our role. And not to be envious of others, or judge them according to what we are called to do. More important, we are not to judge our own activities—or anyone else's—by apparent results. That is not what matters, however much we and the Lord with us want us to do well. The thing that matters is the love with which we accomplish our tasks or role. As one of the great mystics of the sixteenth century put it, "When the evening of life comes, we will be judged on love." How else can a God who is love judge? Therefore, even for those of us who are called to an active ministry within the Body of Christ, it is essential that we do spend enough time at the feet of the Master. We need to nourish our love and establish strongly in our hearts a true perspective so that we do not worry or fret, but always choose the better part, the one thing necessary—the way of love.

6

WHEREVER THE GOOD NEWS
IS PROCLAIMED
There Is a Place for Waste

Six days before the Passover, Jesus went to Bethany, where Lazarus was, whom he had raised from the dead. They gave a dinner for him there; Martha waited on him and Lazarus was among those at table. Mary brought in a pound of very costly ointment, pure nard, and with it anointed the feet of Jesus, wiping them with her hair; the house was full of the scent of the ointment. Then Judas Iscariot—one of his disciples, the man who was to betray him—said, "Why wasn't this ointment sold for three hundred denarii, and the money given to the poor?" He said this, not because he cared about the poor but because he was a thief; he was in charge of the common fund and used to help himself to the contributions. So Jesus said, "Leave her alone; she had to keep this scent for the day of my burial. You have the poor with you always, you will not always have me."

—John 12:1-8

We are in Bethany, one of the more affluent suburbs of Jerusalem, and just over the hill from it. The truly rich live in their palatial homes in the city, the poor in their little houses along the crowded streets. But here there is a certain sense of ease and elegance. The homes have welcoming courtyards and spacious dining halls. Today we are in the courtyard of Martha's house, among the crowd looking in upon the feast being given in honor of the Master.

The feast has drawn a lot of attention. The atmosphere is charged. It is the time of the Passover. It seems half the people of the Jewish nation are converging on the city. It is a time of excitement, always. But this year there is something special in the air. There is a sense that something momentous is about to break forth. Jesus has worked countless miracles, including bringing Lazarus back to life after four days in the tomb; he has preached many profound and challenging truths. Now Lazarus sits at his side, very much alive, enjoying his meal and his notoriety and, above all, the friendship of his Master.

This home within which we stand should really be called Lazarus's house. But since the time he died it has been called Martha's house. There is no doubt she has always been in charge, ever since their parents died. Lazarus's resurrection did not seem to change that. Indeed, what happened to him has been hard to grasp. He surely was dead. And greatly mourned. He was buried before sundown and lay four days behind the great stone, rotting in his tomb. Now, one isn't quite sure whether he is a ghost who might disappear at any moment, or what—though there he is at table, eating and drinking like any other ordinary mortal. Rumor has it that the enemies of Jesus are out to kill the risen one—his liveliness is too hard to overlook or deny.

Martha is very much in evidence, fluttering about as always, very busy, seeing that all are well cared for. And Mary, the beautiful one—there she is now. There have been many stories about her. She seemed to have disappeared for a time. Perhaps it was the overbearing control of her older sister, especially after the death of her parents. Or perhaps her head was turned by her own stunning beauty. Report had it that she was carried off to Magdala by some handsome, fabulously wealthy young merchant from afar. Later, abandoned there, she had to fend for herself in the streets.

There has been talk about her first encounter with the Master—the haughty, licentious Magdalen becoming a chaste penitent. But is the fabled Magdalen really our Mary? And then, the incident at Simon's house, when the woman of the streets was preferred over the proud Pharisee—her love proclaimed in the forgiveness of sin. That caused quite a stir.

Here she is now, once again at the Master's feet. This time she has no need to wash those sacred feet. With joyous excitement, her brother Lazarus had carefully washed them when his much loved and revered Guest arrived at his door. Yet tears of joy do run down her shining face as Mary lovingly works the rich ointment, soothing feet well callused by the roads of Judea, Samaria, and beyond. The broken flask, alabaster though it be, lies discarded on the ground.

Mary held back nothing. She had no time to let the rich ointment pour out, precious drop by precious drop. She abruptly fractured the vase and let all its richness gush out upon her Beloved. The scent filled every corner of the house. We are heady with its powerful aroma.

There seems to be a bit of commotion at the table. One of the Twelve is standing. His face is contorted. There is anger in his eyes. "Why this waste? This could have been sold for three hundred days' wages. How much we could have done for the poor!"

There are poor among us in the courtyard. We will all have to push our way through the beggars, the blind and crippled, when we enter the Temple on the morrow. My own heart stirs a bit. I look around at the poor here. But they don't seem to be disturbed. The poor often have a sense of magnificence about them. They love the Master. They are happy to see him extravagantly honored and cared for. Nor does this outspoken one arouse much sympathy among the other disciples at the table. They know their Judas. What a sham is his outcry! He is not concerned about the poor, only about filling the purse he carries. How sadly true it has always been that some of the voices raised for the poor are hardly sincere, and the speakers drive away in their Cadillacs. But still, we wonder about the prodigality of fracturing an alabaster jar and pouring out thousands of dollars worth of perfume.

Now the Master speaks. He who expressed such love and care for the woman at his feet when she came to him in Simon's house has not changed. "Leave her alone. She has done a good thing." Jesus-God does want us to waste on him. Certainly, he was not unmindful of the poor. The poor best knew that. No rabbi had ever so identified with the marginalized: born in a stable, rushed into exile, a poor hard-working carpenter from "Hicksville," the son of a widow. He first blessed shepherds and later invited fishermen and tax collectors to be his intimate and chosen friends. He touched lepers! as well as the blind and the crippled and others who had every sort of disease. He fed the hungry. He is indeed the Master of the poor and outcast. Yet, as the poor so well know, there is a time and place for prodigality. He, the Holy One, had intimately accepted the love of a prostitute. Could she ever be too extravagant in the expression of her love? Never.

Jesus wants our extravagant love; he wants us to pour out on him personally something of the richness of the life he has given us. Through prophetic voices, he had depicted his desires as a love affair. I have often thought of this as I have listened to a not-uncommon tale one hears in marriage counseling. The husband is miffed, hurt, uncomprehending. He cannot see why his wife is not satisfied. He has done so much for her. He has been working night and day. He has given her a beautiful home and a house in the country, vacations in Florida and Maine. She has furs and jewels, her own Cadillac. What more could she possibly want? When he has finished his long, self-righteous litany of labors of love, his wife adds but one tearful line: "If only he would give me himself once in a while." I sometimes imagine God leaning over the balustrade of heaven, shaking his head, looking down at his busy, devoted disciples: "If only they would give me themselves once in a while." God does want us to pour out some of the precious ointment of our lives on him once in a while.

The apostolic and primitive Church considered this word to be an extremely important one. Matthew quotes Jesus as saying: "I tell you solemnly, wherever in all the world this Good News is proclaimed, what she has done will be told. . . ." John places it in a prominent position, just before the recounting of the great Paschal mystery. He does not often repeat something that is fully reported in the other, earlier Gospel accounts. In his report here, he emphasizes the presence of the risen Lazarus, Jesus' greatest miracle prior to his own resurrection, which it prefigured.

The fragrance of what Mary did filled the whole house, lifting all there to new levels of experience. The intimate communion of contemplative love is a perfume in Jesus' house, the Church and his world. A contemplative dimension is meant to make each one's life more fragrant in giving witness to the divinity and humanity of Christ—the Anointed One—our God. The contemplative life of certain communities of men and women is a fragrance among the People of God to remind us all of the importance of this dimension.

Jesus speaks here of the Good News. We want to listen to it with the greatest of care so that its goodness can permeate and inform every aspect of our own lives. A wonderful, prominent Christian woman once shared with me the story of her "conversion." She had been baptized as an infant and brought up in a nominally Christian home. But Christ had never been a significant presence in her life. She was elected to the House of Representatives of the United States. One day, after an exhausting debate, she entered the cloakroom and sought to slip by two of her colleagues to get her coat and be off. As she passed them, she heard one of them say: "We can count on the Lord to take care of that." Without thinking, she blurted out: "God, I wish I could say that." It was a prayer that God heard and the colleague overheard. He replied: "Go home and take out your Bible and read the Gospels the way you would read a bill you have to vote on in Congress, and you will be able to say that."

My friend did. She went home, took the Bible down from where it had long been crammed in among many other unused books, blew the dust off the top, and began to read. She read every word; she read above the words and below the words and before the words and behind the words and in between the words. She questioned and challenged. And soon she was looking for a man of God to lead her into a deeper union and communion with Christ.

A while ago, I was given a poem entitled "Fish." It opened: "What was Jesus doing while they were pulling in the nets?" You immediately recall the scene. Jesus had been pressed by a crowd on the lake shore, so he called Peter's boat into service—prophetic of the future role of Peter's bark, the Church. After the sermon, our gracious Lord would not let a service go unrewarded. He told Peter what to do. It was against all fisherman's reason, yet Peter had learned to be docile to a higher order of unreasoned wisdom. The result was an immense catch. Soon Peter was at Jesus' feet. What was Jesus doing while they were pulling in the nets? Our answer may tell us more about ourselves than about Jesus, but we do need to ask such questions as we listen to the Scriptures.

The question that comes up for me as I listen to the Scripture we have in hand is this: Where did Mary get this fabulous jar of perfume? Lazarus was a good brother and quite well-to-do, but I wonder if he was that well-to-do and that wonderful. It more likely was something that the exotic woman of Magdala might have bought to lure customers. Or the pay of some merchant prince, enamored by the beauty of the woman of the streets who had pleased him so well. If that be the case, what does it tell us about Jesus, that he would accept such a gift? It says to me that no matter what has been our track record, no matter how much sin has been woven into our lives, he still wants us to pour out our lives' love on him. He does not withdraw himself from intimate and loving contact with sinners. Rather, when we come to embrace him in heartfelt prayer, he proclaims to all: "She has done a good thing."

" . . . for the day of my burial."

In the midst of the joyous love and loving joy of this feast, Jesus interjects a piercing note. This anointing of love is for his burial. He has spoken in detail to his Twelve in times past. He would be betrayed, handed over to the Romans, scourged, and crucified. Now he tells them clearly the time is near at hand. The morrow would be a very heady day for his disciples. As he would lead them over the hill toward Jerusalem, at the head of a large band of pilgrims, they would behold an immense crowd coming out to meet him. They would commandeer an ass. Excited men would begin cutting down large palm branches and waving them wildly, while others would throw their cloaks on the ground before the donkey's feet. Even the children would join in the cries of exaltation. But Jesus knew what was in the hearts of people. Within forty-eight hours, one of his very own would be selling him to his enemies for a price far less than the cost of Mary's extravagance. When the climax would arrive, the end would be too violent and abrupt to allow time for a suitable burial service. By instinct—that instinct of the Spirit that leads those who live by love—Mary did now what she would not be able to do then. For by the time she would be able to gather the ointments to care for his dead body, it would no longer be dead, but gloriously risen.

And then she would hear: "Do not touch me." He would

have passed to another state of being. And she would be summoned to another level of union and communion, beyond the carnal or emotion-filled love she had hitherto known.

When we first turn to the Lord, in the hour of conversion, we are often flooded with feelings and emotions that lift us up and fill us with fervor and love. But then our relationship, if it is an authentic relationship with the Lord, leads us up Calvary's hill, and we know the loss when our own very hearts seem to become tombs, empty tombs. When we find him again, there will be a new understanding, a new bonding with him in his mission. Mary, the sinner, the penitent, the lover, was the first evangelist of the Resurrection.

If tradition can be believed, Mary's life did not end there. She spent years in active mission in the early Church. Then, wearied by her years of generous service and ministry, she was given the freedom to return to her chosen place. He had said it would not be taken away from her. She spent her last years sitting at his feet, filling the whole house of the Church with the fragrance of her contemplative love.

In the end, we are all called to be contemplatives, to enter into deep loving union with Jesus. It is then that even those who have labored long and mightily in apostolic undertakings fulfill their greatest mission among God's People. A disciple of Christ need never fear retirement or the physical diminishments of age. These are a gateway to freedom. They are an invitation to enter into the part of Mary, which will never be taken away from them, not for all eternity.

"She has done a good thing." She has poured out her life, symbolically and literally, in love. "Mary has chosen the better part; it will not be taken from her."

7

IN MEMORY

At the Heart of It All

*As they were eating he took some bread, and when he had said the
blessing he broke it and gave it to them. "Take it," he said, "this is
my body." Then he took a cup, and when he had returned thanks he
gave it to them, and all drank from it, and he said to them, "This is
my blood, the blood of the covenant, which is to be poured out for
many. I tell you solemnly, I shall not drink any more wine until the
day I drink the new wine in the kingdom of God."*

—Mark 14:22–25

Table talk can sometimes be very trivial—though even then
it can reveal much about the speakers. And sometimes it
can be sublime. On the night before Jesus died it reached
new heights of sublimity beyond which it can never ascend
in this world of ours. We have traditionally called this meal
"the Last Supper." It was not to be the last meal, or even
supper, that Jesus would eat with his disciples, though it
was the last in the course of his life as a mortal man—a man
who would die. However, it is perhaps most properly called
the "last" because it does reach the ultimate level of
importance.

The heights and depths of the conversation at this meal
are unparalleled. Here we hear of the most perfidious act

that would ever mar the human race. A man would sell out his friend, and such a Friend, for thirty paltry pieces of silver. Here, too, we hear of a love beyond telling. A divine heart opens itself, and we hear of the love that has ever dwelt within the very bosom of the Trinity, the Love of the Father for the Son, that Love who, in unity of substance, is the Holy Spirit of God. We are summoned to enter into that Love and let it be our Love, a Love that makes us one with God, even as the Son is one with the Father. We, of course, cannot understand what all this means. The wonder of its reality will be filling us with inexpressible delights for all the unending ages to come. We can but say yes and let such love invade our being.

However, at this meal things went beyond words. The Host, as any Jewish host might, took bread into his hands and said the blessing. But then he said words that only profound faith can fully accept, words that lesser faith has sought to explain away in whole or in part, words that fulfilled a saying that had sent most of his disciples away from him. He said: "Take and eat. This is my body." Then he took a cup, his last cup (he refused even the numbing cup proffered him on Calvary), and again he broke through all human rationality. "This is the cup of my blood, the blood of a new and everlasting covenant." All was complete now in sacramental ritual. The rite of the Seder had been brought to its ultimate completion. On the morrow, when the reality was complete, he would cry out, "It is finished."

We do not know for certain whether this meal which Jesus celebrated with the Twelve on the night before he died was in fact the Seder meal, the meal of the Passover. The Gospel narratives seem to give conflicting evidence. If it were a Seder meal we can locate this rite of completion most precisely. At the beginning of the Seder, the host breaks one of the pieces of unleavened bread and places it aside. At the end of the meal, this piece that was saved from the first bread blessed and broken is shared as a completion.

After it is eaten, nothing more is to be eaten, for the fullness of the ritual has been attained. On this night it has indeed been attained. Beyond this banquet there can be only the heavenly feast of which this is the supreme sacrament.

In this feast we are nourished and purified with the blood of a covenant. We are set afire—as wine fires the blood and sets the brain reeling. We are brought into the ecstasy of divine union. The great mystics, such as Teresa of Avila, tell us that the mystical marriage between Christ and the Christian is always consummated only at the moment of receiving the Eucharist. Here, baptism is brought to its completion.

Recently I had the privilege of assisting at the baptism of a little girl, Katerina Demetroula, in the ancient rite as it is still preserved and practiced in the Eastern Christian Churches. It was very graphic and rich. The child was met at the door of the church, and Satan was forcefully commanded to depart from her. After three such exorcisms, Katerina was asked three times, "Do you accept Christ?" Then, "Have you accepted Christ?" Only then was she brought within the temple, stripped of all her clothing, and thrice immersed totally into the consecrated waters. Buried with Christ and rising again, Katerina was then anointed all over with the unction of the Spirit. Finally, having been clothed in white garments and given the light of Christ (a lighted candle), she was brought before the royal doors, and the priest came forth with the Eucharist. The Christed one communed with Christ.

Who can deny, when they witness such a baptism, that every Christian is called to the most intimate of unions with God in Christ? Unfortunately, human traditions have torn asunder what God has meant to be together. In some Churches, the reception of Christ in the Eucharist is prohibited until years after baptism. In other Churches, the reception of the Eucharist is so hedged around with penitential and preparatory rites that adults rarely approach the sacrament of union. Jesus has said: "Let the little ones come to me, and forbid them not." He had said, "Come to me, all you who are heavily burdened." The traditions are, no doubt, inspired by reverence. But does love understand such reverence?

Jesus had said: "He who has bathed needs only to wash his feet." Eucharistic celebrations usually begin with a penitential rite. That is enough cleansing for those who have given their hearts to the Lord. Byzantine Christians have the rites of the narthex to prepare them to enter into the community gathered within the temple. Roman Catholics take holy water as they enter their churches, thereby renewing their baptism, being cleansed again with the sign of the cross.

Jesus gave no thought to fasting at the last Supper. When the Bridegroom is present, it is not the time for fasting. He served the Divine Food right with the ordinary.

We do need to be purified. But Jesus has purified us already, completely, on Calvary's hill. We have but to accept his gift. We have already fasted our forty days with Jesus in the desert. All has been accomplished for us in our Head, into whom we have been baptized. We need but to be the child who accepts all from the Father—the prodigal who takes the path homeward. The Father will rush out. As Jesus depicts him, he has no time even to hear our confession. He immediately calls forth the robe of the firstborn and adorns us with it. Let us not, like that envious and aggrieved firstborn, unworthy of so great a father, seek to restrict or limit the Father's overflowing love. Our sense of sin and of unworthiness should never hold us back from this feast—that is *not* God's will. Like the prodigal son, we need to come to ourselves and realize that we are, by baptism, truly the children of God. "Can a mother forget the child of her womb? Yet I will not forget you." If we but turn to him and allow him, he will cleanse us, clothe us, and rejoice to have us at his feast. We are children of the household. We belong at our Father's table. We are, by baptism, one with the Son. In this meal, the oneness is renewed and consummated. Each Communion makes this oneness more complete as it draws us more and more into alignment with the mind and heart of Christ.

The monks of old saw pride as the primary vice. If we want to stand on our own and not be the children of God, God will not feed us and care for us, for we block out all possibility of grace and divine life. But this was not the primary problem for the monks, as it is not for most Christians. The primary problem is rather the vice they called *accedia*—spiritual sloth. We do not stir ourselves to respond to the values of our life and our call.

This is why spiritual reading is such an important part of Christian life. Faith comes from hearing. The Christian community incorporates into the Eucharistic celebration the Liturgy of the Word. The reading of the Scriptures, the breaking of the Bread of the Word, is to prepare us, to stir up in us desire for the Bread of the Eucharist. If we do not find in ourselves a certain longing to eat the Eucharistic Bread and drink the Cup, we need to renew our faith by some serious reflective reading on the Eucharist, beginning with the Gospel texts.

This *accedia* is common enough. The Eucharist is so available that we can let it become common and unappreciated. I suffered from this myself some time ago—or rather I became aware of how I was affected by it. When I did not find a book that stirred my sluggish soul, I set about writing one: *The Eucharist, Yesterday and Today*. They say that the best way to learn something is to teach it. Perhaps the best way to read something is to write about it.

We do need to keep renewing our Eucharistic faith. This mystery is so incredible to the human mind. After the striking miracle of the multiplication of the loaves, Jesus broached this idea, unveiling, as we would say, his plan to institute the Eucharist—to give his own body as food. Remember the reaction of his disciples? They "no longer walked with him." So Jesus turned to the chosen Twelve: "Will you also go away?" At that point, Peter had one of his finer moments: "Lord, to whom shall we go? You have the words of eternal life."

These are "the words of eternal life":

I am the bread of life.
He who comes to me will never be hungry;
he who believes in me will never thirst. . . .
Your fathers ate the manna in the desert
and they are dead;
but this is the bread that comes down from heaven,
so that a man may eat it and not die,
I am the living bread which has come down from heaven.
Anyone who eats this bread will live for ever;
and the bread that I shall give
is my flesh, for the life of the world. . . .
I tell you most solemnly,
if you do not eat the flesh of the Son of Man
and drink his blood,
you will not have life in you.
Anyone who does eat my flesh and drink my blood
has eternal life,
and I shall raise him up on the last day.
For my flesh is real food
and my blood is real drink.
He who eats my flesh and drinks my blood
lives in me
and I live in him.
. . . anyone who eats this bread will live for ever.

—John 6

In the early Church it was unthinkable that the Christian community would come together and not all would partake of the Eucharist. The practice even grew for the faithful to take home a portion of the Bread to nourish themselves daily in the family. Through ensuing centuries, exaggerated ideas and tepidity of faith and desire took their toll. It is a long, complicated history, but the end result was that the

Eucharist ceased to be daily bread or even weekly bread. It became the rare encounter for the occasionally prepared.

The Roman Catholic Church broke through this when the saintly Pontiff Pope Pius X restored frequent and daily communion. The Second Vatican Council continued this process, till now it is most common for all to receive at each Eucharistic celebration. However, the Roman Catholic Church does still withhold the Eucharist from its littlest members. The Orthodox Church, happily, invites each one to Eucharist from the moment of baptism. It is a common sight in an Orthodox church to see babes in arms and little rascals being brought to the Holy Doors for the Food of Life. Sad to say, few adults follow them. A demanding practice of preparation still holds them back, though more and more the great spiritual leaders of Orthodoxy are urging frequent Communion. When little Katerina Demetroula received Communion for the first time, I would like to have seen her very devout father and mother and her godparents (at least they, if not all who were sharing in the welcoming of this little one into the communion of the faithful) receive with her.

Other Christian Churches have their own particular practices in regard to the Eucharist and the frequency with which it is celebrated. But I would encourage all to listen more deeply to the Lord in the Scriptures. Listen to his command: "Do this in memory of me." Listen to his words in John's Gospel, Chapter 6. Then ask: Is our practice a wholehearted response to the Lord?

"Do this in memory of me."

We wonder how much the disciples understood at this moment. Who can understand this mystery, except by the Spirit who teaches us? Jesus promised that the Spirit would come to teach us everything and to remind us of all he has taught us. But at that moment of institution, what did it mean to them?

Did at least John understand? Stored deep in his heart were those words Jesus spoke on the morrow of his great picnic. Jesus' words that day were a scandal to most of those who had crowded into the synagogue at Capernaum to hear him. But Peter gave voice to the faith of the Twelve. They believed, but they did not know quite what it all meant or how it was to be. Now they knew.

Jesus went on: "Do this in memory of me." This moment of first Communion was not to be a unique moment. From that day forth, Jesus' followers were to be nourished in the Breaking of the Bread. Even as he "took bread, blessed and broke it and gave it saying, 'Take, eat,' " so his disciples, in his name and memory, in obedience to this his command— nearly his final command before he ascended the cross— would, through the ages, "take bread" and say, "This is my body." We eat so that we may live forever and be raised up on the last day.

Just as on that memorable day at Capernaum, many still say, "This is intolerable. Who can accept it?" They quickly explain it away: "Jesus didn't mean this is really his flesh and blood. It's only a symbol. It's to make us think about him and how he wants to nourish our lives." But the faithful, like Peter, say, "We believe. We know that you are the Holy One of God." We do not understand how bread becomes your flesh, wine your blood—you are ever the glorified Lord. But we believe. And we eat your flesh, looking forward to the promised eternal life.

Sometimes (probably more than we realize) it is better to stop talking, and even thinking, and just *be* in the Reality.

8

IN THE BREAKING OF THE BREAD
Were Not Our Hearts Burning?

Two of them were on their way to a village called Emmaus, seven miles from Jerusalem, and they were talking together about all that had happened. Now as they talked this over, Jesus himself came up and walked by their side; but something prevented them from recognizing him. He said to them, "What matters are you discussing as you walk along?" They stopped short, their faces downcast.

Then one of them, called Cleopas, answered him, "You must be the only person staying in Jerusalem who does not know the things that have been happening there these last few days." "What things?" he asked. "All about Jesus of Nazareth," they answered, "who proved he was a great prophet by the things he said and did in the sight of God and of the whole people; and how our chief priests and leaders handed him over to be sentenced to death, and had him crucified. Our own hope had been that he would be the one to set Israel free. And this is not all: two whole days have gone by since it all happened; and some women from our group have astounded us: they went to the tomb in the early morning, and when they did not find the body, they came to tell us they had seen a vision of angels who declared he was alive. Some of our friends went to the tomb and found everything exactly as the women had reported, but of him they saw nothing."

Then he said to them, "You foolish men! So slow to believe the full message of the prophets! Was it not ordained that the Christ should suffer and so enter into his glory?" Then, starting with Moses and going through all the prophets, he explained to them the passages throughout the scriptures that were about himself.

When they drew near to the village to which they were going, he made as if to go on; but they pressed him to stay with them. "It is nearly evening," they said, "and the day is almost over." So he went in to stay with them. Now while he was with them at table, he took bread and said the blessing; then he broke it and handed it to them. And their eyes were opened and they recognized him; but he had vanished from their sight. Then they said to each other, "Did not our hearts burn within us as he talked to us on the road and explained the scriptures to us?"

They set out that instant and returned to Jerusalem. There they found the Eleven assembled together with their companions, who said to them, "Yes, it is true. The Lord has risen and has appeared to Simon." Then they told their story of what had happened on the road and how they had recognized him at the breaking of bread.

—Luke 24:13–35

Part of the journey for the disciple of Christ is the downhill journey from Calvary. Each of us has our moments in Gethsemani. If we do not run away, as our forebears did that first Gethsemani night, we will then be led on, through one of those painful but grace-filled, dying-to-self experiences. Then there is a certain numbness. We are wrung out. The Christ in us seems quite dead. The resurrection of faith and hope has not yet taken place in our hearts.

This is not the moment when we want to meet one of those Spirit-filled Christians, all aglow with joy. Even a steady self-confident one is a little hard to take. Our response to such might well be, "You must be the only person staying in Jerusalem who does not know." Jerusalem is, of course, the Church. Anyone who stays a while in the Church, in the fellowship of Christ, knows well such times of death, of dying to self. It is part of the journey. The saints have written about it. Some of them have called it the dark night. But all their descriptions sound much too eloquent for our own death experience. We can only say, "We had hoped." But now we are tempted to walk away from it all—and may well be on our way.

It is then that we need someone to come along—someone who knows, because he or she has searched the Scriptures. Someone who, because he knows by experience, is compassionate and will walk with us at our pace and open for us the Scriptures.

"He explained to them the passages throughout the scriptures . . . "

I sometimes think we Christians are apt to limit ourselves too much to what we call the New Testament. Saint Peter assured us that *all* Scripture was written for our instruction. In Isaiah, in those powerful passages that so graphically describe the Suffering Servant, details of our Lord's Passion are filled in for us.

> Without beauty, without majesty (we saw him),
> no looks to attract our eyes;
> a thing despised and rejected by men,
> a man of sorrows and familiar with suffering,
> a man to make people screen their faces;
> he was despised and we took no account of him.
>
> And ours were the sufferings he bore,
> ours the sorrows he carried.
> But we, we thought of him as someone punished,
> struck by God, and brought low.
> Yet he was pierced through for our faults,
> crushed for our sins.
> On him lies a punishment that brings us peace,
> and through his wounds we are healed.
>
> We had all gone astray like sheep,
> each taking his own way,
> and [the Lord] burdened him

with the sins of all of us.
Harshly dealt with, he bore it humbly,
he never opened his mouth,
like a lamb that is led to the slaughterhouse,
like a sheep that is dumb before its shearers
never opening its mouth.

By force and by law he was taken;
would anyone plead his cause?
Yes, he was torn away from the land of the living;
for our faults struck down in death.
They gave him a grave with the wicked,
a tomb with the rich,
though he had done no wrong
and there had been no perjury in his mouth.
[The Lord] had been pleased to crush him with suffering.

—Isaiah 53:2–10

As we let these words sink in, along with passages from the Psalms and the Gospel narratives, we begin perhaps to see some of the meaning of our sufferings, of our death experiences. Paul had said that we are to "fill up what is wanting in the passion of Christ." A mysterious saying. Can there be anything wanting in the Passion of Christ? We have been baptized into Christ, made one with him in a oneness that is beyond anything we can ever fully comprehend. What is wanting in the Passion of Christ is its physical, human presence in our world here and now. It is made present when it is lived out in our lives. We make the healing and love of Jesus' Passion present and efficacious among his people when we experience it in our lives.

This is one thing we learn when the Scriptures open for us. And our hearts begin to burn within us.

But it is not the only thing. We hear, too, the fact and the promise of resurrection. And our hope is rekindled. We begin to be ready to find our Lord again in the breaking of the bread. Our eyes are opened.

There is yet more. The Scriptures entice us into that reality of which the communion in the broken bread is but a sacrament. Let us read again the Song of Songs. Let us hear—really hear—that sentence from Hosea: "I will lead her into the desert and there I will speak to her heart." Then we will know what our downhill journey from Calvary, our dark night, our time in the desert, is all about. We will understand the full meaning of the breaking of the bread only when we experience it in the context of those utterances that poured forth from the heart of our Lord when he first took bread and broke it for us.

When we walk that downhill road from Calvary and know the emptiness of that first Holy Saturday, when faith seems to reside only in the heart of the quiet one who pondered all things in her heart, we need the companionship of the Lord; we need him to open the Scriptures for us. The Lord does dwell in his life-giving Word. We have but to open the Bible and he is present, ready to make things clear for us, to renew our faith and set fire to our hearts.

Unfortunately, it is at these moments when we most need to hear the Word that we are prone to walk away from Jerusalem, the Church, and the hearing of the Word. This is why it is so important for Christians to become habituated to sharing the Word. If we are accustomed to sharing Scriptures with our Christian friends, then surely, as we begin to walk away, one or the other of them will catch up with us and begin to share the Word with us. We will not get very far. And we, too, will often enough be the Lord catching up with some of our brothers and sisters as they head downhill with dashed hope and darkened spirits. But in these moments, when it befalls us to be the Lord to the one on the road to Emmaus, let us be sure not to seem to be the only one in Jerusalem who has not known Gethsemani, Calvary, and the road beyond. Let deep compassion always be at the heart of our faith sharing, especially with those who faith and hope are seemingly in the past tense.

"They . . . recognized him in the breaking of the bread."

With the background of this lesson in Scripture, with the renewing of their faith and the uplifting of their hope, Cleopas and his companion were ready to recognize the Lord in the breaking of the bread.

If we do not really experience Jesus in the Eucharist, if it is not a moment of transforming encounter for us, then perhaps we have not yet opened our minds and hearts sufficiently to the Bread of the Word. In her celebration of the Eucharist, the Church always begins with a banquet of the Word. Faith comes from hearing. Our faith does need to be renewed. But this short renewal, just like the brief penitential rite, is not always enough for us. "He who has bathed needs only wash his feet." But if it has been a while since we have bathed ourselves in the Word of God, we perhaps need more. No one can really prescribe for each of us how much time we need to spend with Jesus in the Scriptures to keep our hearts aglow. We alone can be the judges of that. We simply need to be honest with ourselves. "Is my heart aglow?" If it is not, then obviously I need to make more time for the Lord, to let him open to me the revelations of his love. If I do not truly recognize the Lord in the breaking of the bread, then I need more time with the Lord in the Scriptures. It is as simple as that.

"They set out that instant. . . . "

When our hearts are burning within us, when we encounter the Lord in the Breaking of the Bread, we cannot but desire to bring this joy, this empowerment, to others. When we love someone, that person's desires and aspirations become ours. Jesus cried, "I have come to cast fire on the earth, and what would I but that it be enkindled everywhere?" His word is fire. These two on the road away from the Church suddenly found a most pressing desire to bring their joy to the Church. What if it was darkening? What if they had walked all day? They had seen the Lord. And they had a most urgent need to bring this Good News to others.

Our Master has told us that the second great command, like unto the first, is that we love our neighbor as we love ourselves. Enkindled with that love of God-Christ, which fulfills the first command, and knowing their own intense joy, love of neighbor impelled their steps up the road to Jerusalem. For once, an ascent was easier than a descent—for love frees us from the gravitational pulls of this world. The love of Christ urges, impels, carries us along. Freely have you received (how great is the Divine largesse, even to downhill sinners!); freely give.

And what did they find in Jerusalem?

They had left without faith or hope—"We had hoped. . . ." Sometimes we do need to go apart from the community of the faithful. We are driven out, out into the desert. I think the Lord allows this so that we can come face to face with the darker side of our being. We grapple with our unbelief; we learn to pray: "Lord, I believe; help my unbelief." We grapple with our despair in the face of our infidelity or in the face of God's seeming infidelity; we learn to pray: "Even though he slay me, yet I will praise him." We are led on the downhill journey into the desert, and he speaks to our hearts. Then we can return to the Church with a renewed faith. And with our story we support and strengthen our brothers and sisters.

The Church that greeted Cleopas and his friend when they burst into the upper room was very different from the one they had left not too many hours ago. The community had had their experience in the person of their leader: "The Lord has risen and has appeared to Simon." The currents of joy flowed into each other. The difference that Cleopas found in the group, though, was in great part due to the difference in him. A few hours later, after even greater communal experience of Christ, Thomas would accept nothing of the communal experience. He closed his heart to the joy his community had found in its renewed hope and belief. Often the problems we see in the Church truly have their roots in ourselves, in the way we perceive things. When we are ready to criticize the community or feel a bitterness rising in our hearts against our sisters or brothers, let our first reaction be to move along the path in which the Spirit mysteriously led Cleopas. Let us go apart for a bit, walk with the Lord in the Scriptures—find a companion for the way, if we can—until our hearts begin to burn. When we are ready, let us join in the Breaking of the Bread, truly recognizing the Lord in our midst. Then let us return to the community with our witness of faith, renewed hope, and joy. And see if we do not find a different community.

Let us not live out of reaction, especially to the weeds that Jesus promised would always be among his wheat till the final harvest. Let us live out of the creative forces of faith, hope, and love within ourselves, nourished by Communion with our Eucharistic Lord. Let us not come to the community expecting it to do everything for us. Let us come with joyful witness, wanting to share from the abundance we have so gratuitously received.

We will all have our downhill journeys. Unfortunately, for most of us, there will be more than one. We hang on and are not willing to die, once and for all, to the false self. That false self rises up with the new person and continues to plague us. We will have to die and rise again and again. But each time we find ourselves on the downhill road on the other side of Calvary, let us invite the Lord to walk with us in the Scriptures, and when he has set our hearts ablaze again, let us hurry back to the Church for the Breaking of the Bread.

9

GHOSTS DON'T EAT

But a Risen Savior Does

*Jesus himself stood among the disciples and said to them, "Peace be
with you!" In a state of alarm and fright, they thought they were seeing a ghost. But he said, "Why are you so agitated, and why are these
doubts rising in your hearts? Look at my hands and feet; yes, it is I
indeed. Touch me and see for yourselves; a ghost has no flesh and
bones as you can see I have." And as he said this he showed them his
hands and feet. Their joy was so great that they still could not believe
it, and they stood there dumbfounded; so he said to them, "Have you
anything here to eat?" And they offered him a piece of grilled fish,
which he took and ate before their eyes.*

*Then he told them, "This is what I meant when I said, while I
was still with you, that everything written about me in the Law of
Moses, in the Prophets and in the Psalms, has to be fulfilled." He
then opened their minds to understand the scriptures, and he said to
them, "So you see how it is written that the Christ would suffer and
on the third day rise from the dead, and that, in his name, repentance for the forgiveness of sins would be preached to all the nations,
beginning from Jerusalem. You are witnesses to this.*

*"And now I am sending down to you what the Father has prom-
ised. Stay in the city then, until you are clothed with the power from
on high."*

—Luke 24:36–49

It had been quite a day. In fact, the most significant day in
the history of the world. As Paul would later say, "If Christ

79

be not risen, our faith is in vain." But this day he has risen from the dead, proclaiming his victory over sin and death.

Let us enter the upper room and join the Twelve—now the Eleven—and try to enter into their experience. As the day opened, there was a jumble of emotions among them and within each heart. Certainly, profound sorrow and shame. They had lost their Master, the man they had come to love more than any other. For him they had left home and family and all their possessions. But, sad to say, in the last moment they had left him and fled for their own safety. On top of these emotions there was fear. Now that the Sanhedrin had had its way with the Master, what might it do to his disciples? It was the women who went out to complete the burial rite; the men cowered behind locked doors.

Deep down there was some inkling of hope. He had said he would die—and he did, even to detail, in the way he had said he would. He had also said he would rise on the third day. The prophecy was clear enough and sufficiently well known for the Jewish authorities to take precautions against it, or at least against a fraudulent claim of it. For who could guard against a resurrection? There was some reason for hope in the hearts of the disciples.

And then came the confusing events of the day. The breathless Mary of Magdala, excitable woman that she was, and filled with love and grief, had come back with tales of angels and an empty tomb. Peter and John had rushed out, leaving the others even more fearful and confused. Then the women arrived with their report of seeing Jesus on the path. Later, Peter returned. He did not have much to say. But he had seen the Lord—Peter had seen the Lord. This was the most credible witness. Considering his state, the state of a man who had three times denied his Master, there was no doubt he had seen someone or something.

Then Cleopas and his companion returned. They had left early that morning. They had hoped, but their hope moved into the past perfect tense. It was over for them, and they left the Eleven and the community to return to their village and their former lives. Now they were back with their exciting story: the opening of the Scriptures, the breaking of the bread.

And then . . .

There he was. In the midst, though the doors were still firmly bolted. He was familiar, yet different. Certainly, very different from the haggard man who rose from Gethsemani's rock, his face soaked with bloody sweat—the last time most of them had seen him. What was in his face now?—so serene, so luminous yet not, certainly not, the brilliance of Tabor that had once blinded. Each searched it from the emotions of his own heart. Did he expect anger at betrayal, pity at cowardice, mirth at such human folly, transcendence (for this was a risen One)? What are our expectations as we look upon the face of Christ? How do they color our perceptions? Do we allow Jesus to be Jesus to us? Does he have to work hard to get us to accept him for who he is?

Jesus-God, their risen Lord, spoke the word: "Shalom—Peace be with you!" How much they needed it! How much do we need the peace of the Risen One! His gentle gaze penetrated right into the depths of their minds and hearts, as easily as his body had passed through the locked doors. Once before they had imagined him a ghost—that night after the picnic, when he had stayed behind to pray and then had come across the water in the third watch of the night. That time a rambunctious Peter had proposed his own test. But now, a new Peter, who had been transformed by a glance, made no such bold gesture.

Jesus took the initiative. He held out his hands. Large, gaping wounds stood fresh and red in the middle of the wrists. He raised his robe, and all could see the gashes in his feet. He realized that seeing was not enough for them. "Touch me. . . . Feel with your own hands my wounded hands. I washed your feet; now embrace my wounded feet. Believe me, my brothers. Please believe me." I wonder if any dared to step forward. If the Magdalen was there, she would have been quickly at those feet. But she did not need the proof. She already knew. Her love was enough to tell her the reality, so the consolation of the feet was denied her.

Still, Jesus' manifestation was not enough. Can you blame the Eleven? Maybe. They had seen three resurrections. Why could not he who had raised the dead raise himself? Perhaps the jeer of the Sadducees was still echoing in their minds: "He saved others. Himself he cannot save." Himself he could not save, for that was not the way of love at that moment, and love is the supreme law, always. But he could raise himself, for that was the way of love. And raise himself he did.

"Have you anything here to eat?" And he "ate before their eyes." How often had they shared a meal! How important it is for friends to share a meal, to break bread! This communion in the neediness of our humanity—how it feeds our relationship! Now the Risen Friend would enter again into this basic human communion, even after he had left the human way of mortal life that needed to be so sustained. He let them serve him. It would be their gift of food. He would be the receiver. They would know well that it was the food of the ordinary person. A piece of grilled fish. This Divine Fish, the *ICHTHUS*, grilled on the fire of the wood of the cross, took their humble offering of fish. This time he would not bless and multiply it to fill many empty stomachs. Rather, he would eat it himself to fulfill the hope in those who surrounded him and to take away the emptiness that death had left in their lives.

Their eyes were fixed upon him as he bit into the fish in the old familiar way. They watched him chew, and the swallowing. The fish was truly consumed, and so was their doubt. I suspect then that those who had held back when he urged them to touch now rushed forward, all seeking a place in his expansive arms. He was indeed their Jesus, their Master. He was here, he was risen. Now they could touch those sacred wounds and weep and kiss them.

What can enable us to break through and accept Jesus in our lives as he really is? God's greatest struggle is to get us truly to accept his overwhelming, totally gratuitous love. It is precisely that—overwhelming. And we do not want to be overwhelmed. We want to stay in charge. We do not want to be the little ones who accept all, openly and unashamedly. We want, too much, to stand on our own two feet and earn our own way. Even when we let that go, such gratuity is unbelievable. We have no comparable experience. We can only open ourselves to Jesus' love that comes to us through others. We can only open ourselves again and again to the mystery of Holy Communion. And hope that, eventually, the reality of his gratuitous love will break through. Then we will be able to break away from all the doubts of a rational mind and throw ourselves into his arms, surrendering to a love that overcomes the deadliness of our sins and the closedness of the tomb that proclaim to us our unlovableness and our unlovedness.

The Master then began to explain it all to them. It was all there in the books they had known since childhood. Moses, the Prophets, the Psalms they had sung together—all told of what was to come. It was obvious now. Those who were with him on Mount Tabor should have seen. But those who were with him there were the ones who came closest to him in his dark hour and were seared most deeply. Yet they were the ones who, at the first report of an empty tomb, ran in response. Opening the Scriptures is the key. Insofar as each of us opens the Scriptures regularly, we are prepared for the resurrections of Christ in our own lives. He dies in us, again and again, as periods of consolation and light give way to times of darkness, trial, and uncertainty. Floods of questions pierce our hearts as we hang on the cross of faith and hope. We need to return, again and again, to the Scriptures, ardently praying that he will open them to us and that we will see. Above all, that we will see the immense gratuitous love of God for us in the Passion, death, and Resurrection of our Lord Jesus Christ, truly present in our own lives.

This is the Good News, this is the hope, the only hope of the human heart. How much it needs to "be preached to all the nations"! But our preaching, our sharing of the Good News, will be credible only if we are indeed witnesses. But we can truly give witness only to what we have experienced in our own lives. When the Scriptures live in us, because the risen Christ lives in us, then we can effectively speak the word of salvation. We must see and experience the one who is of sin in us die and the new life of love arise. What happened in baptism, in sacramental reality, when we were buried with Christ in the waters and rose new persons in the Risen Christ, has to be a lived experience in our lives if we are to give witness.

So Jesus did not send the Twelve immediately out to give witness, to spread the Good News. Rather, they were to "stay" until they were clothed with power from on high. We must not be too eager to begin our ministries, to convert others, or even to help and console. First, we must "stay." We must stay with the Lord until we do have a lived experience of death and resurrection within ourselves. Like Paul, we must come to know in whom we believe. Even when Paul had his dramatic conversion experience and Jesus spoke to him personally and he was enlightened by the Church in the person of Ananias, he still needed his time in the desert. He had to "stay" until he was clothed with power, the power that converted the nations and enabled him to pay such a price in that labor.

Traditionally, priests are to be prepared for their ministry by some years apart in a seminary; religious are to have their time of novitiate. In the freneticism of our times, the years of the seminary have been shortened, and more and more has been crowded into them. There is little "staying" left in them. The same is true of the novitiate. No wonder the priesthood and the religious life have become so fragile and appear so powerless in the face of the world. Priests and religious have been going forth before they are clothed with power from on high. They have not allowed themselves the time to experience death and resurrection. They cannot give witness to what they have not experienced. If the Church does not refind this important dimension of priestly and religious formation, fewer and fewer will want to enter upon what is seen as an ineffective ministry. And those who do enter will suffer ever-greater frustration, which will lead to burnout or defection or refuge in sad compensations.

On the day of his resurrection, Jesus promised to send the Spirit. He fulfilled his promise not long after. And we know the transformation and empowerment that came upon these poor, cowardly fishermen. Jesus never fails to keep his promise. And that promise abides with the Church till this day. If only we will "stay," if only we will seek and long—seek, and you shall find—we will be clothed with power from on high. Not to want to be empowered from on high is a real failure on the part of any Christian. We are to love as we are loved. Our depths should long to bring the Good News in power to all our brothers and sisters in any way we can. For this, we need to be empowered from on high. For one accepting the call to ministry within the Body of the Church, not to seek and long for empowerment from on high is an almost unbelievable contradiction. It is as sad perhaps as that exercise in supreme frustration that marks the lives of those who devote their God-given genius to creating the nuclear weapons they devoutly pray will never be used. To devote our lives to ministry without empowerment from on high and without being able to witness from personal lived experience is a comparable squandering of the talents and gift of a beautiful human life.

We all need to learn how to "stay" until we are empowered from on high. We all need to learn how to sit in quiet prayer with Mary, who sat in the midst of the disciples, pondering all these things in her heart. Out of the inner experience of dying to self and rising to a new life in Christ, we will give credible and powerful witness. Looking upon us, people will be able to see, to touch, and to feed upon the Lord. He will not be a ghost for them, but a living reality in us, in our love, in our power.

10

DO YOU LOVE ME?
A Prophecy Reversed

Jesus showed himself again to the disciples. It was by the Sea of Tiberias, and it happened like this: Simon Peter, Thomas called the Twin, Nathanel from Cana in Galilee, the sons of Zebedee and two more of his disciples were together. Simon Peter said, "I'm going fishing." They replied, "We'll come with you." They went out and got into the boat but caught nothing that night.

It was light by now and there stood Jesus on the shore, though the disciples did not realize that it was Jesus. Jesus called out, "Have you caught anything, friends?" And when they answered, "No," he said, "Throw the net out to starboard and you'll find something." So they dropped the net, and there were so many fish that they could not haul it in. The disciple Jesus loved said to Peter, "It is the Lord." At these words "It is the Lord," Simon Peter, who had practically nothing on, wrapped his cloak around him and jumped into the water. The other disciples came on in the boat, towing the net and the fish; they were only about a hundred yards from land.

As soon as they came ashore they saw that there was some bread there, and a charcoal fire with fish cooking on it. Jesus said, "Bring some of the fish you have just caught." Simon Peter went aboard and dragged the net to the shore, full of big fish, one hundred and fifty-three of them; and in spite of there being so many the net was not broken. Jesus said to them, "Come and have breakfast." None of the disciples was bold enough to ask, "Who are you?"; they knew quite well it was the Lord. Jesus then stepped forward, took the bread and gave it to them, and the same with the fish. This was the third time that Jesus showed himself to the disciples after rising from the dead.

After the meal Jesus said to Simon Peter, "Simon son of John, do you love me more than these others do?" He answered, "Yes, Lord, you know I love you." Jesus said to him, "Feed my lambs." A second time he said to him, "Simon son of John, do you love me?" He replied, "Yes, Lord, you know I love you." Jesus said to him, "Look after my sheep." Then he said to him a third time, "Simon son of John, do you love me?" Peter was upset that he asked him the third time, "Do you love me?" and said, "Lord, you know everything; you know I love you." Jesus said to him, "Feed my sheep."

> *"I tell you most solemnly,*
> *when you were young*
> *you put on your own belt*
> *and walked where you liked;*
> *but when you grow old*
> *you will stretch out your hands,*
> *and somebody else will put a belt around you*
> *and take you where you would rather not go."*

In these words he indicated the kind of death by which Peter would give glory to God. After this he said, "Follow me."

Peter turned and saw the disciple Jesus loved following them—the one who had leaned on his breast at the supper and had said to him, "Lord, who is it that will betray you?" Seeing him, Peter said to Jesus, "What about him, Lord?" Jesus answered, "If I want him to stay behind till I come, what does it matter to you? You follow me."
—John 21:1–22

Peter was not the only one who denied Jesus. But this blustery, thick-skinned, rough man had to experience betrayal more profoundly, more rudely, than the others. But they all had betrayed their Master. They all had run away. Except, maybe, John. John, perhaps, had just quietly melded into the crowd and continued to follow his Master, right into the high priest's house, through the trial, and on to Calvary. He was always there. For he was the disciple whom the Master loved. We must never forget that it is Jesus' love for us,

God's creative love for us, that makes us faithful, just as it is that love that makes us to be and to be loving and to love. All is pure gift. John was perhaps the simplest, the most naive, the youngest of the disciples. He was the one whose heart was wide open to let the divine love pour in and create in him being the disciple whom Jesus loved and who loved. He knew, as he preached ceaselessly in his last years, that the fullness of the Gospel lay in love. "Little children, love one another. Little children, love one another."

This whole question of betrayal was part of the drama of the Last Supper. After Jesus had humbled himself and washed the feet of every one of them, including the betrayer, he told them the sad fact that one of them would betray him. While all the others, with a certain uncertainty about themselves, with a certain humility, pointed to themselves and asked, "Is it I, Lord?", the self-assured Peter turned to the disciple whom Jesus loved, who even then was resting his head on Jesus' bosom. Peter signaled to him and whispered, "Find out who it is." Peter was sure it was another.

Even when Jesus singled Peter out and told him of Satan's designs upon him, Peter insisted vehemently, "Lord, I am ready to face imprisonment and death itself, rather than deny you." Then Jesus bluntly foretold that Peter would indeed deny him, and deny him three times, that very night before the first glimmers of dawn called forth the cry of the cock.

The event we now witness, John tells us, is Jesus' third appearance as Risen Lord to his disciples. At the first one, on Easter night, Jesus did indeed share a "meal" with them. He accepted from them a bit of their grilled fish and ate it in front of them, trying to reassure their fearful spirits, their tenuous faith, and their lingering hope. He was not a ghost, but truly their Risen Lord. His second appearance was a special one for the doubting Thomas. How Jesus accommodates himself to our weaknesses and our needs! He stood there again, his hands stretched out, his feet clearly displayed. He even opened the side of his robe and let the great gaping wound that led into his heart stand in plain evidence. "Thomas, come. You asked for tangible proof. It is yours. Put your finger into my hand. Put your hand here, into my side. Believe, my dear one, believe." How good and how gracious is our God!

This third appearance by the side of the sea was for the group as a whole. It was to be indeed a meal of reconciliation. We have seen that Jesus was rarely the host at the meals that are reported. He was host at the first great picnic and at its follow-up. He was host at the Last Supper, when he served a meal beyond human comprehension. Now in this moment of complete reconciliation he was again the host. Bread was prepared, fish was somehow caught and put to roasting on the coals. And yet, with that great delicacy that was his, not all the fish. He would allow his disciples to make their contribution to the meal. The Lord gives us everything. Certainly, all the fish the disciples caught were the gift of the Lord's bounty. And yet, in giving us all, he graciously accepts back, as part of his work of re-creation, our humble offerings. Indeed, our God is a gracious God!

Jesus' invitation to this meal is a curious one. First of all, there is the name by which he called his disciples. The Greek word is difficult to capture in English. It does connote friendship, but it also connotes something else, sometimes translated as "children." It is used by a benign elder speaking to the younger members of the community. Perhaps it is the spiritual father who is coming forth here, one who is going to call forth the younger ones to a fuller sharing in the life of the Spirit.

Then Jesus asked them: "Have you anything to eat?" He was ready to provide for them, to provide for the basic needs of life. He was ready to host them at a gracious morning meal after their long night of toil. There are many resonances here. These are fishermen. Again, they have known a night of fruitless toil. Coming from him, what a reminder of other times when he, with a word of direction, used their obedience to turn their fruitlessness into a bountiful catch! One wonders why all seven did not immediately recognize the Lord. If they were too far out to see him clearly, his directive, which proved so fruitful, should have immediately caused them to sense who had spoken to them. The account makes us realize that it is only the eyes of one who loves that perceive the Lord: in himself, in others, and in his creation. It was the disciple whom Jesus loved who first recognized Jesus.

Again, there is also emphasis on the leadership of Peter. When the beloved disciple did recognize the Lord, he turned first to Peter. It was for Peter, the leader, to authenticate the recognition and to lead the rest to Jesus.

Peter had undergone a profound transformation that moment when the glance of Jesus pierced to the very depths of his being and laid bare to him all his weakness and yet told him how much he was loved. But his impulsiveness was not completely gone. In a moment, he was in the water, plunging, thrashing, rushing forward. This time he did not have the foolhardiness to ask the Lord to let him walk over the waters. He just let love drive him forward through the obstacle of water until he found the feet of the Master he loved. He did not cry out now in some kind of incipient humility, "Lord, depart from me, for I am a sinful man." The Lord had departed from him up Calvary and down into the tomb. Peter knew the desolation of that departure. He wanted never to experience it again. No, now he let love take over. He plunged to grasp the feet of the Master he loved.

The others followed along in the boat, towing the great net of fish. Perhaps this is the way it should be in the Church. The leader, the successor of Saint Peter, should be that great charismatic figure who stands forth in all his weakness as a man like the rest, and yet a man who burns with an impetuous love for Christ and plunges ahead and shows the way, while the other apostles follow along, care-

fully bringing the whole flock of Christ, the whole catch of
his love. It is still clear, even though Peter plunged ahead
through the water to the feet of Jesus, that it was Peter's
catch. In the end it was he who took hold of it and brought
it ashore to the feet of Jesus. There is much for us to reflect
upon and assimilate here in coming to understand respective roles in the Church in the service of Christ and in the
ministry to his people.

There followed the beautiful meal of reconciliation. Jesus himself, the Lord and Master, took the bread, broke it,
and gave each one a portion. Stooping over the fire and
gathering up the fish, which he had so carefully grilled, he
saw that each one had all he wanted. Again, an important
lesson for us who are called to minister, to lead God's people, to be other Christs. It was completely clear now to the
disciples that if the betrayal had ever caused some kind of
space to open between them and the Master, some kind of
rift in their relationship, it was now totally healed, left behind, forgotten. For most of us the big problem with sin and
failure is that we find it so hard to forgive ourselves, even
after God has forgiven us. We find it difficult, as Saint Paul
says, to forget what is behind and to press forward. God's
forgiveness is complete, but we unfortunately tend to mea-
sure it by our own poor, oftentimes half-hearted, forgiveness. How often I have heard someone say, "I forgive, but I
never forget"! Is that forgiveness? God, in his infinite love
and compassion, does forgive and forget. Indeed, God lives
always in the joy of the complete reconciliation, sanctifica-
tion, and glorification of each one of us. The more we can
practice wholehearted forgiveness, the more we will be true
to who we are: men and women made in the image of God.

Peter's betrayal of Jesus had been unique. The others had
run away, fleeing for their lives. They had placed their own
safety and well-being before their loyalty. They had indeed
betrayed the Lord. Now he had forgiven and had drawn
them to himself again in the intimate communion of a

meal. But Peter, always special in his relations with Jesus, had not so betrayed the Lord in running away that his love failed to draw him to turn back and follow along. Yet in the end he betrayed the Lord with words, oaths, and curses.

Now the Lord, in his immense compassion and healing love, will give Peter a similarly unique opportunity to be reconciled, restored, and reestablished, through words. The chastened Peter will not resort to oaths, certainly not to curses. Rather, he will rely on his Master's infinite, penetrating knowledge. In his first question, Jesus perhaps puts his finger on Peter's tendency to brag and boast. "Simon son of John, do you love me more than these others do?" There would certainly have been a time when Peter would have said, "Of course I love you more than they do." At the Last Supper he had said, "Even if they all betray you, I will never betray you." But it was a different Peter who answered now. "Yes Lord, you know I love you." He is not for making any comparisons. He is only trying to state what he perceives in his own heart, and with a humility that realizes that Jesus knows him better than he knows himself. Jesus gives to the lion who has become a lamb the commission "Feed my lambs." Only the one who has learned from Jesus to be meek and humble of heart can be worthy to serve with him as shepherd of the flock.

In the second question, Jesus does not bring up the comparative element. He just asks simply and straightforwardly, "Simon son of John, do you love me?" Again Peter meekly and humbly answers, "Yes, Lord, you know I love you." Then Jesus amplifies his commission, "Tend my sheep." The Fathers of the Church have, in their interpretation of this response, seen Jesus' commissioning Peter here not only to be shepherd of the flock, but also to be shepherd of the shepherds, to be the leader of the other disciples, as he had so naturally been through the years of public ministry and even now in these days of the Risen Lord.

Jesus went on then, almost relentlessly, it seemed: "Simon son of John, do you love me?" The third question cut deep, for it brought home to Simon precisely what was going on. His threefold denial burned deep within him. Now he was called to make a threefold affirmation of love so that purifying love might totally exorcise every remnant of the betrayal from his heart.

With greater humility than ever before, Peter affirmed that the truth did not ultimately reside in him, but in Jesus, who is the truth: "Lord, you know everything; you know I love you."

Peter had reached the depths of humility and of truth. He no longer depended at all on himself. He depended wholly on Jesus. So he was ready to take Jesus' place at the head of the disciples as his risen Lord departed for the heavenly places. "Feed my sheep."

The compassion and goodness of our Lord seem to be absolutely without end. He who once had the pain and sorrow of telling the man whom he so deeply loved the prophetic word that he would be a traitor, now turns that all around. With healing love he gives voice to another prophecy. In Jesus' compassionate love there must have been a certain joy, and at the same time a certain pain, in this prophecy. A joy, because the prophecy told of fidelity, of union with him, and of likeness to him. At the same time, a certain pain, because he loved this man and would be with him in his pain and suffering. In healing words, Jesus contrasted the past with the future: "I tell you most solemnly, when you were young you put on your own belt and walked where you liked." It was this self-will of Peter, even as a disciple, that got him into so much trouble. How many of us are self-willed in our discipleship? We follow Jesus and do the things he wants, no so much because he wants them, but because we want them. We have decided that this is the meaning we want to give to our lives; this is the way to make a difference; this is the way to get ahead in the values, in the institution, in the life we have chosen for ourselves.

The true Christian disciple, who is like his Master, seeks rather to do always the things that please the Father. The acts done by these two different kinds of disciples might seem very much the same. But God looks on the inner heart. How much of our apostolic zeal is true self-giving love? How much of it has about it a certain self-aggrandizement? This is a question which perhaps we all need to ask ourselves at times. One of the early Fathers placed as the first goal of Christian life the achieving of purity of heart. If the essence of Christian life is love, then this is the first goal: to come to live and act and labor out of love.

When Peter was young, he did the things that pleased himself, even in following the Lord. But the Lord's grace had now worked through his faults and his failures and his sin to bring him to a purity of heart. Jesus could now prophesy of him: "When you are older you will stretch out your hands, and another will tie you fast and carry you off against your will." Then Jesus added: "Follow me."

He indicated how Peter would die, just as at times he had foretold his own death with its handing over, scourging, and crucifixion. Peter was to die a death very similar to his Master's. The important thing, though, was that in that death he would follow Jesus. He would accept all that would happen and live through it, because it pleased the Father, because it was what Jesus wanted, because it was what Jesus had done. Peter, even in the prophecy of his death, was being summoned to the fullness of perfect discipleship. We know, in the event, that he accepted that invitation and lived it to the full.

The disciples of Jesus form a community, a close-knit community. Indeed, a community that is knit so close that it is called and is, in some way, the very body of Christ, who is our head. One of the things we lay hold of to excuse ourselves from living our discipleship to the full is within that very community. We make others within the community the norm of our own discipleship, rather than keeping our eyes fixed on Christ, letting him, in his perfect obedience and submission to the Father and in his total, self-giving love, be our sole model and Master. It is not, perhaps, that we really want an excuse. It is very much in the fabric of our human nature that we want others with us. We do not want to go it alone. We do not want to stand out in the crowd, to be isolated persons. Yet when it comes to the bottom line, each of us is a unique expression of the divine Love, uniquely loved by God. Each of us has, ultimately, a unique vocation. We have to have the courage to be who we are and to express Christ and Christ's love in our own unique way.

This moment when Peter was being called to ultimate and unique discipleship, he instinctively reached out. He saw the disciple whom Jesus loved and whom he loved. He wanted him as companion on the ultimate way. Did not Jesus send them together to prepare the Last Supper? Had they not been bonded since the days of the first call? "What about him, Lord?" Will he be with me all the way? Is he, too, called to this complete discipleship?

Jesus' response seems almost heartless: "What does it matter to you?" It could easily be misunderstood. Are we not supposed to be concerned about our brothers and sisters? Are we not in some way their keepers? Jesus is not denying this. He is just underlining a truth with that strong, prophetic exaggeration which on another occasion went so far as to say that we must hate our father and mother, brother and sister, and even our own life. When it comes to complete discipleship, we must be ready to forget everybody else and simply and totally follow Jesus. "You are to follow me." At Cana, where for the first time we encountered Jesus and his disciples together at a meal, we saw Jesus gently summoning them forth to faith and confidence in him. The journey since that meal had been a long one. In many ways, a very difficult one. It had had its joys and it sorrows, its heights and its depths. Now, in this last meal he would share with them on earth, the summons is to the completion and consummation of that to which faith and confidence in him would call them—to complete discipleship, to follow him both in that sign of perfect love—"Greater love than this no man has than that he lay down his life for his friend"—and in that depth of inner purity of heart: "I seek always the things that please the Father."

Our first call to follow Christ at the moment of conversion is just a beginning—a beginning of a wonderful and yet totally demanding journey. If we constantly keep close to Christ and listen to him, little by little he will reveal himself to us and draw us forth in faith and love. Until finally he gives us that fullness of grace that creates in us such a likeness to him that we are ready to follow him to Calvary for no other reason than that this is what pleases the Father. We want to be like him in that, seeking to do only what pleases the Father. "Not my will, but thine be done, Father."

This is the rite of passage, the only way by which we can be adequately prepared to enter into that unending communion with Christ in God which is best described as the heavenly banquet, the nuptial feast of the Lamb. There we shall sit at the heavenly table and for all eternity feast upon the Word, in deepest intimacy of human and divine love. This is what we are called to. This is what we have been made for. This is why Jesus taught us so often through the medium of the meal and all that can surround it. Let us make this the sole objective of our lives: to be worthy to participate in this heavenly banquet through oneness with Christ and with all the others who are invited to share at this table. We seek a oneness that expresses itself in love and caring and in a like-mindedness, in a common concern to do only the things that please the Father, to do all we possibly can to bring this creation to that unity and fullness that is the design of our infinitely loving Father.

11

SIDE BY SIDE

The Consummation in the Kingdom

"Write to the angel of the church in Laodicea and say, 'Here is the message of the Amen, the faithful, the true witness, the ultimate source of God's creation: I know all about you: how you are neither cold nor hot. I wish you were one or the other, but since you are neither, but only lukewarm, I will spit you out of my mouth. You say to yourself, "I am rich, I have made a fortune, and have everything I want," never realizing that you are wretchedly and pitiably poor, and blind and naked too. I warn you, buy from me the gold that has been tested in the fire to make you really rich, and white robes to clothe you and cover your shameful nakedness, and eye ointment to put on your eyes so that you are able to see. I am the one who reproves and disciplines all those he loves: so repent in real earnest. Look, I am standing at the door, knocking. If one of you hears me calling and opens the door, I will come in to share his meal, side by side with him. Those who prove victorious I will allow to share my throne, just as I was victorious myself and took my place with my Father on his throne. If anyone has ears to hear, let him listen to what the Spirit is saying to the churches.' "

—Revelation 3:14–22

In my pseudo-sophistication—seen to be quite pseudo in my moments of greater light—I have tended to pooh-pooh much of popular piety. But in the moments of light I remember my grandmother with her little prayer books and many prayers who, in the way she lived, taught me that the Christian life added up to something far more significant than prayer books, church services, and ritual fasts. She was full of the wisdom of a Desert Mother with her own words of life: "Always leave the table a little hungry." "Never go to bed with an 'I'm sorry' unsaid." And I remember my mother. The rosary was her prayer. It led her and helped her be a woman of deepest faith, abiding contentment, and unending love and care.

I have to admit that the excitement I felt as I set sail for Patmos at least bordered on popular piety.

The cruise out was interesting enough—certainly beautiful as we made our way through the translucent blue of the Aegean. At each island it seemed that all the thousand youth who were packed around me on deck passage flowed off, only to be replaced by another thousand going on to the next island. When we arrived at Patmos at two in the morning, I joined the landward flow. The next day I wondered, for not one bedraggled youth was in sight.

It seemed as if I had been transported back through the centuries. The great fortress monastery on the crest of the island dominated everything—a refuge against invading Turks. (The Turkish mainland can be seen in the distance.) The little houses that lined the roads leading to the monastery—all roads led there—were too white in the strong sun, something from the travel agent's poster. All the churches seemed to be filled to overflowing as ancient chants flowed over the heads of the congregations and into the sunny plazas spread out before them. As I looked from the roof of the fortress, I could see farmers plowing with their horses, yokes of oxen patiently treading the mill floor, thrashing the wheat, and hundreds of bunches of grapes on the roofs, drying for the raisin market. Time had not altered the pattern of life here.

The island was undoubtedly less populated when John,

the beloved of the Lord, lived here in exile. I had to search among the houses to find the gully-like path that led down to his cave. The little church that now surmounts the cave is hardly more significant than the surrounding houses. Within, signs marked the respective niches: here John slept, here he prostrated in prayer, here he sat as he dictated the Book of Revelation. With enough piety to do justice to any popular devotion, I sat in that latter niche and opened the Book of Revelation. And for the first time it opened itself to me, some passages more than others—the one we have listened to together, more than any other.

In one of his delightful little stories that pack so much infinite wisdom, Jesus had once compared his kingdom to a marriage feast. The munificent Father had prepared the feast for his Son and sent out many invitations. But the invitees were too busy about other things to respond. One had new oxen to try out, another had a new wife, the third a new farm to see. The heavenly Father invites us to the everlasting nuptials of his Son, where he takes to himself his bride, the Church, born, like Eve, from his side as he slept upon the cross. But the same excuses reach the Father. We are too busy about our possessions, about our lives and our lusts, about our own earthly land, to respond to his invitation.

Then the Father is said to have sent out his servants, commanding them to go to the highways and byways and "compel" the invitees to come in. Not that the Father would ever force those to whom he has given freedom, but he wants his apostles and disciples and all his messengers to press his invitation as strongly as they can.

There is a well-known story about a famous painting of this scene from Revelation where Jesus stands at the door and knocks. When the artist first displayed it, the critics quickly jumped upon what they thought was a glaring omission: there was no latch on the door. But the artist knew what he was doing: "This door opens only from the inside." Jesus, in his own person and in the persons of his many beloved disciples, constantly knocks at the door of our hearts. But he will never force it open.

If we do open, what a wonderful experience awaits us! John depicts it from his own experience at the Last Supper and on other occasions. The Lord will come in and sit down with us, to enjoy a most intimate meal for two—two intimate friends. We will not sit on opposite sides of the table, but side by side. Like John, we can rest our heads upon the bosom of Christ and hear the beating of his heart. This may all sound rather saccharine, but anyone who has been truly in love knows the delights of an intimate meal with the Beloved, and the even greater delight of cradling one's head on a welcoming breast and listening to the beating of a heart so loved and loving. God, who made us humans, knows our deepest feelings and aspirations—even when we ourselves do not.

We recall the rest of our Lord's little story. Among those who were "compelled" to come in was one who did not have a wedding garment. So the poor man was bound hand and foot and cast out into exterior darkness. We fear.

Jesus has obviously got our number. He knows we are not burning with that fervent love for the Father that marks his whole life. "I seek always to do the things that please the Father." Nor are we cold, or we would not be involved in this relationship at all. The fervent One can not but feel a certain nausea at our tepidity. And he expresses his feelings quite graphically. Yet he is not stopped by his feelings. We ourselves have many feelings we would perhaps rather not have. We need to admit them honestly, face their reality, and then let them go. We do not need to let them dictate how we are going to act. Like Jesus, we can go on to foster positively the situation that will respond to our aspirations and give us joy. I may feel very cool toward my brother or even resentful, yet I can be friendly so that we can work together for our common good.

To the lukewarm, "wretchedly and pitiably poor, and

blind and naked too," Jesus offers to supply the wedding garment, the wedding gift, all that we need. It is ours for the price of love.

"Those who prove victorious. . . ."

My inclination, as I read this text, was to say, "Some victory!" All we have to do is open the door, and he does the rest. But that is the reality. All we have—even our victories—are ultimately his free gift. We have but to receive it from him.

And what a victory! We are brought right into the glory of the Trinity: "Those who prove victorious I will allow to share my throne, just as I was victorious myself and took my place with my Father on his throne." We are back to the Trinitarian mysticism that Jesus first opened to us at the Last Supper: "May they all be one, Father, may they be one in us, as you are in me and I am in you." We are called to a oneness with Christ in God that brings us right into the very glory of the Trinity. Yet in this oneness with God we never lose our uniqueness. The Lord has a profound respect for the work of his hands.

In the medieval church of Santa Maria in Trastevere in Rome there is a very special mosaic. Usually, when we see Jesus with his mother, he is a babe in her arms, or she is standing at the foot of his cross. We do have the exceptionally beautiful Pietà, where Jesus is again in his mother's arms. But in Trastevere we see the fulfillment of the this prophecy and promise from the Book of Revelation. There, in the apse, we see Mary sitting beside her son on his throne—with an added note of exquisite charm: Jesus has his arm around his mother. This mosaic was produced in the middle of the twelfth century when, for the first time, a Cistercian sat on the throne of Saint Peter in Rome. Mysticism and humanism came together in the lives and writings of the great men who first articulated the Cistercian spirit.

Mary, in her complete yes to God, is a model for us; she shows us the way to victory. Mary knew herself well. She knew she was the lowly handmaid of the Lord. And she also knew that he who is mighty had done great things for her. Even as she proclaimed her own exaltation, she assured us that his mercy extends from generation to generation to those who fear him. Like Mary, when we see ourselves reflected in the eyes of Love, we know how good and blessed we are. Yet we fear, for we know, too, our sin and our proclivity to sin yet again. This very fear wins for us his mercy.

Ultimately, the message and the life meaning we receive from the table talk of Jesus is that of his great love for us and his desire to share a table with us forever at that banquet in his kingdom. There each of us can, if we wish, be the disciple whom Jesus loves, resting our head on his bosom, enjoying fully and constantly the love of the Sacred Heart.

> Out of his infinite glory,
> may he give you the power through his Spirit
>   for your hidden self to grow strong,
> so that Christ may live in your hearts through faith,
>   and then,
> planted in love and built on love,
> you will with all the saints have strength to grasp
>   the breadth and the length,
>   the height and the depth;
> until, knowing the love of Christ,
>   which is beyond all knowledge,
> you are filled with the utter fullness of God.

Christianity is a religion of joy and victory. Jesus stayed but three hours on the cross and three days in the tomb. As Risen Lord he stayed forty days in our midst and then ascended gloriously to reign forever in the heavenly kingdom. His coming had been heralded by the joyous salutation of an angel. Mary had quickly brought sounds of joy to her cousin, and the babe in Elizabeth's womb leapt for joy.

Then the heavens broke open as its joy was shared with shepherds (a marginalized people) and all the earth. The consummation of it all, for us all, is the marriage feast of the Lamb, with its endless sounds of joy.

We are a people of resurrection. In his resurrection Jesus conquered not only the tomb and death. He conquered the eternal death of sin. He did this not only for himself—for the sinless One hardly needed such a victory—but for us all. At baptism, we are baptized into the death and resurrection of Christ. We go down into the waters *and come up again.* None of us is left submerged in the baptismal font.

We are an Alleluia People.

Do we realize this? Do we live it? Saint Augustine has said well: "The glory of God is a person fully alive."

Some years ago I attanded a *sesshein,* a Zen retreat. The Roshi, the Zen Master who was conducting the retreat, was having his first intimate contact with Christianity. Knowing little English, he studied a bilingual New Testament, reveling in the *koans* of Christ, the sayings of Christ that invited the human mind to break out of its confining categories and to experience transcendent truth. Then he came to the great *koan.* When I visited him that evening, he pierced me deeply with his shining, dark eyes: "You are a Christian. Show me your resurrection. I want to see your resurrection."

That is our challenge, our glory, our joy.

EPILOGUE

Not His Kind of Bread

The disciples had forgotten to take any food and they had only one loaf with them in the boat. Then Jesus gave them this warning, "Keep your eyes open; be on your guard against the yeast of the Pharisees and the yeast of Herod." And they said to one another, "It is because we have no bread." And Jesus knew it, and he said to them, "Why are you talking about having no bread? Do you not yet understand? Have you no perception? Are your minds closed? Have you eyes that do not see, ears that do not hear? Or do you not remember? When I broke the five loaves among the five thousand, how many baskets full of scraps did you collect?" They answered, "Twelve." "And when I broke the seven loaves for the four thousand, how many baskets full of scraps did you collect?" And they answered, "Seven." Then he said to them, "Are you still without perception?"

—Mark 8:14–21

These poor disciples—so slow, so literal-minded! They miss the poetry of life—which is the reality of life: the rich tones of divine love that are expressed in the fruited fields and the laden vines where a devout heart ever feeds. We fail to be the children who enter the Kingdom, who trust that our heavenly Father does know all our needs even before we ask, and will provide for them. He cares for the flowers and

107

for the birds, but we fear he will not provide for us, who are worth more than many sparrows.

Thus we hoard. Think of the great stores of grain and other foods that American taxpayers spend millions of dollars each year to hoard for the future, till they begin to rot and have to be distributed hastily. (Remember the cheese distribution!) All the while, thousands upon thousands starve to death. "Do you not remember . . . when I broke the five loaves among the five thousand . . . and when I broke the seven loaves for the four thousand . . . ?" There should be a strong and effective will on the part of all the disciples and followers of Christ to share the Father's largesse and to bring to an end selfish and wasteful hoarding.

"Be on your guard against the yeast of the Pharisees."

What is this yeast that the Lord is warning us about?

Matthew tells us it is the teaching of the Pharisees and Sadducees. Luke explains it more specifically: "the yeast of the Pharisees—that is, their hypocrisy." Their teaching was all about ritual. They were for outward show, the trappings of true religion. Holiness for them lay in the appearances. They concerned themselves about fasts and ablutions. But Jesus would say: "It is not what goes into the mouth that defiles a man, but what comes out of the heart."

There is no place in Christianity for self-righteousness. It is a contradiction in terms. The only true Christian is the follower of Christ. And Christ is the one who washes feet and feeds the hungry and says: "Learn of me for I am meek and humble of heart."

Listening to Jesus at table, we have not heard all of his message. Many things will be learned only in the doing, in imitating what he, our Master, has done: washing feet, feeding and healing, and spending nights in prayer with the Father. We have learned something sitting at his tables. We can learn more sitting in the synagogues and standing in the Temple court, listening there, too.

If this listening at table did nothing more than lead us to decide to go on listening, this would indeed be good. With Peter, our heartfelt conviction needs to be "Lord, to whom else can we go? You have the words of eternal life." We need to listen. His words will open out for us unto life eternal.

We do need to hear Jesus' warning here: "Be on your guard against the yeast of the Pharisees." We are all too prone to settle for the externals of religion, to go through the rituals. We are too apt to give notional assent to the words of life and not a real assent—the assent that calls forth conversion, new directions, positive action. So prone are we to greet the words of Jesus with an "I've heard them all before" attitude.

As the rabbis say, his word is fire. But often for us, the fire is hidden in the ashes of routine and ritual. We insulate ourselves against its burning. He said, "Seek and you shall find." We need to stir the ashes, to ask the Spirit to blow on the coals, so that their warmth can be rekindled for us and spring into jumping, joyous flames, warming and vivifying our lives.

Not every meal is a banquet or a special celebration. True, there are high moments, times for delicacies and treats. But still, we need our daily bread. We need to nourish ourselves with the staples of life even if they do not always tickle our palates. Each day we need to sit at the table with Jesus and eat the Bread of his Word to nourish the life he has given us. On the days we do not let him break for us the Bread of the Word, our spirits languish. If our lives are not filled with joy and all the other fruits of the Spirit, it is because we do not ask, do not seek. His table is always spread. We want always to keep our Bible spread out before us in our homes, in our offices, in our places of ministry, to remind ourselves of this. Let it be there as a tempting dish filled with enticing morsels, inviting us to nibble constantly and to sit down regularly and eat heartily. There is never a moment when we cannot enjoy, be nourished, and be refreshed by the table talk of Jesus.

Taste and see how good the Lord is!